AF614687

Computer Memory and Data Storage

Edited by Azam Seyedi

Published in London, United Kingdom

Computer Memory and Data Storage
http://dx.doi.org/10.5772/intechopen.104072
Edited by Azam Seyedi

Contributors
Ramtin Zand, Mohammed Elbtity, Peyton Chandarana, Ronald F. DeMara, Allam Abumwais, Mahmoud Obaid, Siddhartha Raman Sundara Raman, Azam Seyedi, Per Gunnar Kjeldsberg, Roger Birkeland

First published in London, United Kingdom, 2024 by IntechOpen
IntechOpen is the global imprint of INTECHOPEN LIMITED, registered in England and Wales, registration number: 11086078, 5 Princes Gate Court, London, SW7 2QJ, United Kingdom

British Library Cataloguing-in-Publication Data
A catalogue record for this book is available from the British Library

Additional hard and PDF copies can be obtained from orders@intechopen.com

Computer Memory and Data Storage
Edited by Azam Seyedi
p. cm.
Print ISBN 978-1-80355-588-1
Online ISBN 978-1-80355-589-8
eBook (PDF) ISBN 978-1-80355-590-4

For EU product safety concerns:
IN TECH d.o.o., Prolaz Marije Krucifikse Kozulić 3, 51000 Rijeka, Croatia,
info@intechopen.com or visit our website at intechopen.com.

Meet the editor

Azam Seyedi holds a master's degree in Electronics Engineering from the University of Tehran, Iran, and a Ph.D. in Computer Architecture from the Universitat Politecnica de Catalunya, Spain. Her research focuses on low-power circuit and system designs, reliability, memory design, and computer architecture. As a dedicated VLSI and computer architecture researcher, she has made significant contributions to the field through numerous publications, including conference papers, book chapters, abstracts, and journal articles. Notably, she was awarded the ERCIM Alain Bensoussan Fellowship in 2017, the Marie Sklodowska-Curie Individual Fellowship in 2018, and the Best Paper Award at the Great Lakes Symposium on VLSI in 2011. Dr. Seyedi is an active member of the Institute of Electrical and Electronics Engineers (IEEE) and High Performance, Edge, And Cloud Computing (HiPEAC).

Contents

Preface

In this book, *Computer Memory and Data Storage*, you will learn about the significant role that memory subsystems play in high-performance processors, the challenges associated with low-power memory designs, and the importance of ensuring data integrity and security in memory design. You will also discover various techniques proposed by researchers to address power consumption concerns and reliability issues. The book is organized into five chapters.

Introductory Chapter: Computer Memory and Data Storage introduces the topic of computer memory and data storage. The author highlights the significant role that memory subsystems play in high-performance processors and the impact they have on the overall energy, area, and performance of modern computing systems. The chapter also discusses the challenges associated with low-power memory designs and the need for techniques that effectively handle reliability issues. The author notes that various solutions have been explored to address power consumption concerns, such as scaling CMOS logic circuits. However, aggressive voltage scaling increases the likelihood of memory failures, making it crucial to implement techniques that effectively handle reliability issues associated with low-power designs.

The chapter also discusses the importance of minimizing power consumption while maintaining high performance and reliability, particularly in mobile devices where battery life is a critical factor. The author notes that Dynamic Voltage and Frequency Scaling (DVFS) is one approach to reducing power consumption, but it can also lead to reliability issues. To address these issues, researchers have proposed various techniques, such as Adaptive Voltage Scaling (AVS) and Dynamic Reliability Management (DRM). The chapter also highlights the importance of ensuring data integrity and security in memory design. Memory errors can lead to data corruption and system crashes, which can have serious consequences in critical applications. To address this issue, researchers have proposed various techniques, such as Error-Correcting Codes (ECC) and memory scrubbing.

Chapter *System-Scenario Methodology to Design a Highly Reliable Radiation-Hardened Memory for Space Applications* provides valuable information on designing a highly reliable radiation-hardened memory for space applications. The chapter focuses on the Nwise radiation-hardened cell, and the system-scenario methodology used to optimize energy consumption while maintaining reliability in cache memory circuits. The Nwise radiation-hardened cell is a memory cell that provides tolerance against single-event and multi-event upsets in memories.

The system-scenario methodology is used to optimize energy consumption in applications with dynamic system requirements. This methodology involves analyzing the system requirements and identifying the most critical scenarios that require the highest level of reliability. The energy consumption of the system is then optimized by adjusting the system parameters to meet the requirements of these critical scenarios. The study presented in this chapter focuses on the use case related to satellite systems and solar activity. The methodology was applied to optimize the energy consumption of a cache memory circuit used in a satellite system that is exposed to solar activity. The study showed that the system-scenario methodology can significantly reduce the energy consumption of the cache memory circuit while maintaining the required level of reliability.

Chapter *A Review on Non-Volatile and Volatile Emerging Memory Technologies* discusses the need to address the reasons behind today's performance bottleneck in modern-day processors. The reasons include long access latency of memory technologies, scalability of memory designs, energy inefficiency incurred by increased performance, and additional area overhead. The chapter reviews different memory designs starting from volatile memory technologies such as Static Random Access Memory (SRAM), Dynamic Random Access Memory (DRAM), and NAND/NOR flash to emerging non-volatile memory technologies such as Resistive Random Access Memory (RRAM), Magneto-Resistive Random Access Memory (MRAM), and Ferroelectric Field Effect Transistor (FeFET) with specific consideration of tradeoffs involving area, performance, and energy.

The chapter begins with an introduction to the Von-Neumann architecture, which is the foundational architecture for high-performance CPUs. The chapter then elaborates on the existing technologies and the solutions proposed in the literature to understand the tradeoffs made between energy, area, and performance. The technologies described are SRAM, DRAM, NAND/NOR flash, RRAM, MRAM, and FeFET.

It classifies memory technologies into volatile and non-volatile memory technologies depending on whether the data is retained in memory in the absence of power supply. From an architectural perspective, processors use caches made of SRAM that are responsible for fast memory accesses and main memory made of DRAM optimized for density/cost. The secondary storage is made of non-volatile memory technologies like NAND Flash and optimized for higher density/lower cost.

It elaborates on the tradeoffs in both 6T and 8T SRAM designs with respect to performance, area, and energy. The 8T SRAM design is proposed to relax the design constraints for read operation and to amortize the cost of a precharge cycle by performing another useful task simultaneously. The chapter also discusses the tradeoffs in DRAM, NAND/NOR flash, RRAM, MRAM, and FeFET designs.

Field Programmable Gate Arrays (FPGAs) have become increasingly important in modern computing systems due to their flexibility and reconfigurability. However, conventional CMOS-based FPGAs have limitations such as high-power consumption and volatility. This is where MRAM technology comes in, providing non-volatility and low standby power. MRAM-based FPGAs have the potential to overcome the limitations of conventional FPGAs and provide a new generation of reconfigurable fabrics.

Chapter *MRAM-Based FPGAs: A Survey* provides a comprehensive overview of the recent developments in the field of MRAM-based FPGAs. It begins by introducing the concept of FPGAs and their importance in modern computing systems. It then discusses the limitations of conventional CMOS-based FPGAs, including their high-power consumption and volatility. The chapter then introduces MRAM technology and its potential to overcome these limitations by providing non-volatility and low standby power.

The chapter provides a comprehensive review of the prior research in the field of MRAM-based FPGAs. The chapter includes a table summarizing the design objectives, architecture, fabrication, speed, area, power, reliability, and security of various MRAM-based FPGA designs over the past two decades. The chapter also discusses the advantages and disadvantages of various MRAM technologies, including Spin-Transfer Torque MRAM (STT-MRAM) and Magnetic Tunnel Junction (MTJ) MRAM. It highlights the potential of MRAM technology to provide non-volatility and low standby power, which are essential for low-power applications such as Internet of Things (IoT) devices. MRAM-based FPGAs can also provide high-speed reconfiguration, which is important for applications such as software-defined radio and cognitive radio.

It also discusses the potential of MRAM-based FPGAs to provide high-security applications due to their non-volatile nature. The chapter then discusses the challenges associated with developing MRAM-based FPGAs. These challenges include the need for new design methodologies, the need for new fabrication processes, and the need for new testing and verification techniques. The chapter also discusses the potential future directions for research in this area, including the development of new MRAM technologies, the integration of MRAM with other emerging memory technologies, and the exploration of new design methodologies.

Chapter *New Content Addressable Memory Architecture for Multi-Core Applications* discusses a new content-addressable memory architecture for multi-core applications. The architecture is designed to address issues that arise when multiple cores try to access the same shared module in the shared cache memory. The near-far access replacement algorithm and the dual-port content addressable memory design are two solutions that are proposed to address these issues. The near-far access replacement algorithm is a new algorithm that is designed to improve the performance of shared cache memory in multi-core processors. The dual-port content-addressable memory design is another solution that is proposed to address issues with shared cache memory in multi-core processors. The chapter also discusses the performance of the new content-addressable memory architecture compared to a set-associative cache memory.

Finally, it discusses potential applications for the new content-addressable memory architecture in the field of massively parallel computation. The architecture is well-suited for applications that require high-speed access to shared memory, such as machine learning and data analytics. The architecture can also be used in other applications that require high-speed access to shared memory, such as video processing and scientific simulations.

Azam Seyedi
Faculty of Information Technology and Electrical Engineering,
Department of Electronic Systems,
Norwegian University of Science and Technology (NTNU),
Trondheim, Norway

Chapter 1

Introductory Chapter: Computer Memory and Data Storage

Azam Seyedi

1. Introduction

Memory subsystems play a significant role in high-performance processors, occupying a considerable portion of the die area. Consequently, they have a profound impact on the overall energy, area, and performance of modern computing systems [1]. This necessitates the development of low-power, reliable, and high-performance memory solutions to cater to the needs of emerging applications.

Various solutions have been explored to address power consumption concerns. For instance, scaling complementary metal-oxide-semiconductor (CMOS) logic circuits offers improvements in power consumption, area utilization, and speed. However, aggressive voltage scaling increases the likelihood of memory failures. Thus, further reducing the supply voltage poses a risk to the accuracy of computations. Consequently, it is crucial to implement techniques that effectively handle reliability issues associated with low-power designs in such systems [2, 3].

Motivated by these challenges, this book focuses on memory designs and explores the techniques to minimize power consumption while enhancing performance and reliability. Readers will gain insights into recent advancements in computer memory and data storage through investigation and analysis. By engaging with this resource, they will stay updated on the latest developments in computer memory and data storage.

2. Balancing performance and energy efficiency in cache memory design: Voltage scaling and power management strategies

Cache design plays a critical role in optimizing memory access efficiency in modern processors [1]. One commonly used type of cache is SRAM (Static Random-Access Memory), which offers fast access times and is commonly employed in cache hierarchies. However, in the pursuit of low-power memory design, innovative techniques are being explored to reduce power consumption in SRAM-based caches. These techniques include voltage scaling, where the supply voltage to the SRAM cells is reduced, as well as adaptive power gating, which selectively shuts down portions of the cache when not in use [4]. By incorporating such low-power design methodologies, cache systems can achieve a balance between performance and energy efficiency, contributing to overall system power savings while maintaining satisfactory memory access speeds [5].

Voltage scaling is a popular approach employed to reduce power consumption in memory subsystems. Operating at lower voltages significantly decreases power dissipation, leading to improved energy efficiency. However, voltage scaling brings challenges such as increased vulnerability to soft errors caused by radiation-induced particle strikes [2, 3]. To counter this, radiation hardening techniques are employed to enhance the resilience of SRAM cells against such errors. These techniques, such as redundant circuitry, error correction codes, and error detection and correction mechanisms, are employed to ensure reliable operation even in radiation-prone environments [6–10].

3. Reliable radiation-hardened memories: Design methodologies and techniques

Radiation hardening is a critical aspect of ensuring the reliability and robustness of electronic systems, particularly in demanding environments such as space applications. In space, electronic systems are exposed to high-energy particles that can cause significant damage and errors [3]. These particles can come from the sun, cosmic rays, and other sources, and they can cause single-event upsets (SEUs) or multiple-event upsets (MEUs) in electronic systems.

If a radiation strike impacts a node of an SRAM cell and modifies its stored data, it results in a phenomenon called Single Event Upset (SEU) [2]. This occurrence takes place when the charge delivered by the particle strike at the affected node exceeds the critical charge, known as Qcrit. Qcrit represents the minimum charge required to alter the data state stored within the SRAM cell [11]. If two or more neighboring nodes collectively receive and contribute to the deposited charge causing a state change, it is referred to as a Multi Event Upset (MEU) [11]. To address these challenges, radiation hardening techniques are employed in SRAM design.

Redundancy is a common approach wherein additional circuitry is incorporated to detect and correct errors. Error correction codes (ECC) are widely used to identify and correct bit errors, ensuring data integrity [7].

Moreover, techniques like triple modular redundancy (TMR) are employed to enhance system reliability [6]. TMR involves triplicating the circuitry and comparing the outputs to identify and correct errors. This redundancy adds an extra level of fault tolerance, ensuring reliable operation in the presence of radiation-induced errors.

Various techniques have been developed to mitigate Single Event Upset (SEU) issues in radiation-hardened memory cell designs [3]. Although conventional solutions such as ECC, DMR [8], and TMR have been used at the architectural level, they suffer from significant area overhead, power consumption, and increased system complexity, making them unsuitable for small memory blocks, particularly at low voltage levels [12]. In contrast, circuit-level techniques offer a more efficient approach by improving SEU immunity without architectural overhead, resulting in reduced area overhead, delay, and power consumption [3, 13–16].

However, previous designs exhibit various trade-offs in terms of SEU tolerance, critical charge, access time, area overhead, and recovery time. For example, some designs offer SEU tolerance but have a low critical charge (Qcrit) [15, 17] or high read access time [18]. Others address SEU tolerance but come with high area overhead [19], while some have limitations in SEU recovery and MEU immunity [14, 15]. Researchers continue to explore new techniques to develop memory cells that can offer improved radiation robustness while minimizing these trade-offs, especially for space applications and other scenarios requiring high reliability and efficiency.

4. Emerging non-volatile memory technologies: Overcoming limitations of existing technologies

Moore's law, which has significantly enhanced computing technology through technology scaling, has also brought about unintended consequences such as the heightened impact of radiation on SRAM cells. This is due to the increased susceptibility of transistors to noise at lower supply voltages and smaller feature sizes [2]. As a result, researchers are exploring alternative approaches to sustain continued scaling endeavors, leading to the emergence of non-volatile memory technologies.

These technologies, such as Flash memory, RRAM, and PCM, offer the advantage of data retention even when power is removed and are used in storage systems, solid-state drives, and embedded systems where persistent data storage is essential [20]. While non-volatile memories like Flash memory have been widely used in various applications, emerging non-volatile memory technologies such as MRAM, FeRAM, and STT-RAM are gaining attention due to their unique properties, such as non-volatility, high endurance, fast access times, high density, low power consumption, and fast write speeds [20, 21].

These emerging technologies have the potential to overcome some of the limitations of existing technologies. However, they also face challenges such as high production costs and scalability issues, which researchers are actively working to address and improve the performance and reliability of these technologies. Thus, the emergence of non-volatile memory technologies represents a promising alternative approach to sustain continued scaling endeavors and overcome the limitations of existing technologies [22].

5. Conclusion

In summary, the design of memory systems encompasses several key aspects, such as voltage scaling to reduce power consumption, radiation hardening to enhance resilience against soft errors, variation-aware design to address process variations, low-power cache design for improved energy efficiency, fault-tolerant memory design to ensure reliable operation, and the adoption of emerging technologies that have the potential to overcome limitations of existing technologies. By incorporating these techniques, memory systems can achieve high performance, low power consumption, resilience to radiation-induced errors, and robustness against various fault conditions, effectively meeting the demands of modern computing applications.

Author details

Azam Seyedi
Faculty of Information Technology and Electrical Engineering, Department of Electronic Systems, Norwegian University of Science and Technology (NTNU), Trondheim, Norway

*Address all correspondence to: azamseyedi2013@gmail.com

References

[1] Hennessy JL, Patterson DA. Computer Architecture: A Quantitative Approach. 6th ed. Cambridge, MA, United States: Morgan Kaufmann; 2020

[2] Lin D, Xu Y, Liu X, Zhu W, Dai L, Zhang M, et al. A novel highly reliable and low-power radiation hardened SRAM bit-cell design. IEICE Electronics Express. 2018;**15**(3):20171129

[3] Seyedi A, Aunet S, Kjeldsberg PG. Nwise and Pwise: 10T radiation hardened SRAM cells for space applications with high reliability requirements. IEEE Access. 2022;**10**: 30624-30642

[4] Kaxiras S, Martonosi M. Computer Architecture Techniques for Power-Efficiency. San Rafael, CA, USA: Morgan and Claypool; 2008

[5] Seyedi A, Armejach A, Cristal A, Unsal OS, Valero M. Novel SRAM bias control circuits for a low power L1 data cache. In: Proceeding of NORCHIP. Copenhagen, Denmark; 2012. pp. 1-6

[6] Sterpone L, Violante M. Analysis of the robustness of the TMR architecture in SRAM-based FPGAs. IEEE Transactions on Nuclear Science. 2005; **52**(5):1545-1549

[7] Bajura MA, Boulghassoul Y, Naseer R, DasGupta S, Witulski AF, Sondeen J, Stansberry SD, Draper J, Massengill LW, Damoulakis JN. Models and algorithmic limits for an ECC-based approach to hardening sub-100-nm SRAMs. IEEE Transactions on Nuclear Science. 2007; **54**(4):935-945

[8] Teifel J. Self-voting dual-modular-redundancy circuits for single event-transient mitigation. IEEE Transactions on Nuclear Science. 2008;**55**(6):3435-3439

[9] Seyedi A, Yalcin G, Unsal O, Cristal A. Circuit design of a novel adaptable and reliable L1 data cache. In: Proceedings of the 23rd ACM International Conference on Great Lakes Symposium on VLSI (GLSVLSI). Paris, France. 2013. pp. 333-334

[10] Yalcin G, Seyedi A, Unsal O, Cristal A. Flexicache: Highly reliable and low power cache under supply voltage scaling. High Performance Computing. 2014;**1**:173-190

[11] Lin S, Kim Y, Lombardi F. Analysis and design of nanoscale CMOS storage elements for single-event hardening with multiple-node upset. IEEE Transaction on Device Materials Reliability. 2012;**12**(1):68-77

[12] Giterman R, Atias L, Teman A. Area and energy-efficient complementary dual-modular redundancy dynamic memory for space applications. IEEE Transactions on Very Large Scale Integration (VLSI) Systems. 2017;**25**(2): 502-509

[13] Seyedi A, Aunet S, Kjeldsberg PG. Nwise: An area efficient and highly reliable radiation hardened memory cell designed for space applications. In: Proceeding of IEEE Nordic Circuits and Systems Conference (NORCAS): NORCHIP and International Symposium of System-on-Chip (SoC). Helsinki, Finland; 2019. pp. 1-6

[14] Jahinuzzaman SM, Rennie DJ, Sachdev M. A soft error tolerant 10T SRAM bit-cell with differential read capability. IEEE Transaction on Nuclear Science. 2009;**56**(6):3768-3773

[15] Guo J, Zhu L, Sun Y, Cao H, Huang H, Wang T, et al. Design of area-efficient and highly reliable RHBD 10T

memory cell for aerospace applications. IEEE Transactions on Very Large Scale Integration (VLSI) Systems. 2018;**26**(5): 991-994

[16] Jung I-S, Kim Y-B, Lombardi F. A novel sort error hardened 10T SRAM cells for low voltage operation. In: Proceeding of IEEE 55th International Midwest Symposium on Circuits and Systems (MWSCAS). Boise, ID, USA. 2012. pp. 714-717

[17] Jiang J, Xu Y, Zhu W, Xiao J, Zou S. Quadruple cross-coupled latch-based 10T and 12T SRAM bit-cell designs for highly reliable terrestrial applications. IEEE Transactions on Circuits and Systems I: Regular Papers. 2019;**66**(3): 967-977

[18] Calin T, Nicolaidis M, Velazco R. Upset hardened memory design for submicron CMOS technology. IEEE Transactions on Nuclear Science. 1996; **43**(6):2874-2878

[19] Pal S, Mohapatra S, Ki W-H, Islam A. Soft-error-immune read stability-improved SRAM for multi-node upset tolerance in space applications. IEEE Transactions on Circuits and Systems I: Regular Papers. 2021;**68**(8): 3317-3327

[20] Chen A. A review of emerging non-volatile memory (NVM) technologies and applications. Solid-State Electronics. 2016;**125**:25-38

[21] Meena JS, Sze SM, Chand U, Tseng T-Y. Overview of emerging nonvolatile memory technologies. Nanoscale Research Letters. Sep 25 2014; **9**(1). Article number: 526 (2014)

[22] Wong HS, Salahuddin S. Memory leads the way to better computing. Nature Nanotechnology. 2015;**10**: 191-194

Chapter 2

System-Scenario Methodology to Design a Highly Reliable Radiation-Hardened Memory for Space Applications

Azam Seyedi, Per Gunnar Kjeldsberg and Roger Birkeland

Abstract

Cache memory circuits are one of the concerns of computing systems, especially in terms of power consumption, reliability, and high performance. Voltage-scaling techniques can be used to reduce the total power consumption of the caches. However, aggressive voltage scaling significantly increases the probability of memory failure, especially in environments with high radiation levels, such as space. It is, therefore, important to deploy techniques to deal with reliability issues along with voltage scaling. In this chapter, we present a system-scenario methodology for radiation-hardened memory design to keep the reliability during voltage scaling. Although any SRAM array can benefit from the design, we frame our study on the recently proposed radiation-hardened cell, Nwise, which provides high level of tolerance against single event and multi event upsets in memories. To reduce the power consumption while upholding reliability, we leverage the system-scenario-based design methodology to optimize the energy consumption in applications, where system requirements vary dynamically at run time. We demonstrate the use of the methodology with a use case related to satellite systems and solar activity. Our simulations show that we achieve up to 49.3% power consumption saving compared to using a cache design with a fixed nominal power supply level.

Keywords: space applications, solar activity, radiation hardening, single event upset (SEU), voltage scaling, system scenario, SRAM design, reliability, Nwise cell

1. Introduction

The memory subsystems are among the main contributors to the total energy consumption, area, and performance of today's computing systems; therefore, there is a critical need to provide low-power, reliable, and high-performance memories for emerging applications. One of the concerns of memory designs is cache memories. Caches are designed to keep frequently used data and instructions close to the processing unit to avoid power-hungry and slow access to main memory. Almost all modern CPU cores, from ultra-low power chips, such as the ARM Cortex-A53 [1] to the highest-end Intel Core i3-1215UL processors [2], use caches. However, caches are known to consume a large portion (up to 30–70%) of the total processor power [3, 4]. On-chip cache size will also continue to grow due to device scaling coupled with increased performance requirements.

Voltage-scaling techniques are well-known techniques to reduce the total power consumption of the caches. Due to the quadratic relationship between dynamic energy consumption and supply voltage, this is worthwhile even if it incurs overhead in other parts of the system. However, aggressive voltage scaling significantly increases the probability of memory failure. Therefore, further reduction of the supply voltage is not possible without the risk of erroneous computations. This problem increases dramatically in environments with high levels of radiation, such as in space, because the systems stay exposed to high doses of radiation strikes for long periods of time and have limited energy budgets [5]. Therefore, adding advanced techniques to deal with the reliability issues during voltage scaling is critical for energy-efficient memory designs, especially for space applications.

A memory fault is typically modeled as a single event upset (SEU) or a multi event upset (MEU), where a single or multiple nodes in a memory cell may change state due to charge deposited by a radiated energetic particle [6]. Design of low-power and fault-tolerant caches has a rich body of work at different design abstraction levels. Circuit-level techniques are used to improve the reliability of each SRAM cell at low-voltage levels. Apart from the standard six transistor (6 T) SRAM cells, 8 and 10 T SRAM cells have been proposed by [7, 8]. These designs have a large area overhead, which again poses a significant limitation in performance and increase in power consumption of the caches. In addition, they do not provide enough tolerance against high radiation strikes in space.

A hardened 10 T SRAM cell called Quatro-10 T is proposed in [9] to provide higher area efficiency and higher reliability in low-voltage applications with larger noise margin and lower leakage current. It uses negative internal feedbacks to improve the immunity of the cell nodes against SEUs. However, it cannot provide full immunity to all SEUs, and some internal nodes may flip during $0 \rightarrow 1$ SEU [10]. The RHBD-10 T cell is proposed with a low area overhead compared to previous radiation-hardened memory cells [10]. However, the proposed 10 T cell suffered from high read access time that may affect its application, wherever high speed is necessary [10, 11]. Furthermore, even if providing SEU tolerance regardless of the upset polarity, the tolerance capability, that is. the radiation-induced charge it can resist, is not high compared to previously proposed cells [11]. Two quadruple cross-coupled storage cells, the so-called QUCCE 10 T and QUCCE 12 T, are proposed in [12]. QUCCE 10 T is a proper cell design for high-speed applications, while the QUCCE 12 T cell is a promising candidate for low-voltage and high reliability. Their SEU tolerance is lower than several previous designs such as [11], though QUCCE 12 T tolerates higher deposited charge at the expense of larger area. Therefore, the proposed cells may be less suitable for space applications that need high cell robustness and low area.

Nwise and Pwise have recently been proposed as two highly reliable radiation-hardened SRAMs cells [11, 13]. Simulation results show that they are competitive cells for radiation-hardened SRAMs to use in various memory blocks for space applications compared to the state of art. Both have the highest level of SEU tolerance capability for the temperature range deployed in space applications. In addition, both have the highest level of the tolerance to MEU. However, all the simulations are done at nominal voltage levels, and voltage scaling has not been addressed in those papers.

Circuit designs proposed in [14, 15] combine data duplication/triplication with error correction schemes to increase reliability while reducing supply voltage. The design can save energy through voltage scaling and ensure reliable behavior in harsh environments, however, with the cost of high area overhead of additional memory cells.

At the architecture level, several schemes have been proposed to save the energy by reducing the voltage while improving the reliability using sophisticated fault tolerance mechanisms, such as block/set pairing [16], address remapping [17], and block/set-level replication [18]. In another set of schemes, various complex error correcting codes (ECC) have been used to protect against both permanent and transient errors while reducing the voltage [19–21].

Some software-level approaches have been proposed that use language extensions to give the programmer the ability to perform relaxations [22]. For instance, a framework is developed to expose hardware errors to software in specified code regions. This allows programmers to mark certain regions of the code relaxed and decrease the processor's voltage and frequency below the critical threshold when executing such regions.

For other parts of the embedded systems domain, the so-called system-scenario-based design methodology has been developed to optimize energy consumption. System-scenario-based techniques [23, 24] enable exploitation of application dynamism through fine-grained run-time system tuning. At design time, profiling is used to determine the behavior of different run-time situations. Run-time situations are then clustered into system scenarios based on similarity in a multidimensional cost perspective, such as execution time, energy consumption, and memory footprint [25]. Optimal platform configurations, such as dynamic voltage, frequency settings, memory configuration, and task mapping, are then determined for each scenario. Furthermore, efficient scenario prediction and switching mechanisms are developed. At run time, according to the current run-time situation and the scenario knowledge, the application and platform are switched to the optimal configuration.

However, little work has been attempted to leverage a combination of hardware- and software-level techniques to simultaneously manage unreliability and reduce power consumption, especially in the electronics space industry. To this end, our work adopts an approach where the circuit and run-time levels of the system cooperate to improve energy and reliability issues. Our main goal is to design a low-power and fault-tolerant cache memory accompanied with a system-scenario-based design methodology, which makes it possible to minimize power consumption by adapting voltage and frequency levels according to a dynamically changing exposure to different doses of particle strikes. The contributions of this chapter are as follows:

1. We present a radiation-hardened memory circuit design, which keeps the reliability during voltage scaling. This design allows us to operate at nominal voltage levels down to low-voltage levels for space applications.

2. We leverage the system-scenario-based design methodology to optimize the energy consumption at run time.

The rest of the chapter is organized as follows: In Section 2, we first briefly review the Nwise cell design details [11, 13]. Then, we move on to the adapted version of the Nwise cell, which can operate reliably during voltage scaling. We describe the schematic details, operational behavior, and address the SEU robustness analysis.

Furthermore, the circuit simulations results, including read and write delay times, read and write power consumption, and robustness simulations during voltage scaling, are presented in this section. In Section 3, we briefly describe the system-scenario-based design methodology and explain how we deploy this methodology in our design. Then, a case study is presented to confirm the applicability of our design in space. In this section, we show how the system-scenario methodology can optimize the power consumption when the system is operating in space. To confirm the usefulness of our proposed method, our memory energy consumption is compared in two cases: when it is equipped with the system-scenario method and when it operates without considering any scenario decision at run time. Finally, Section 4 concludes this chapter.

2. Memory design details

2.1 Cell schematics

The Nwise and Pwise cells have been recently proposed as area-efficient and highly reliable radiation-hardened SRAM cells [11, 13]. However, we will go with Nwise cell in this chapter since it is a proper choice for cache designs.

Figure 1 shows the details of the Nwise cell circuit. The main storage part of the cell is a cross-coupled pair, consisting of transistors N1 and N2. The backup part is another cross-coupled pair consisting of transistors N5 and N6. The Nwise cell, thus, has four storage nodes Q, QB, P, and PB. Transistors N7 and N8 connect BL and BLB to Q and QB, respectively. N7 and N8 are controlled by the word line (WL): when WL is High, N7 and N8 are ON, and read/write operations are done. Two feedback paths (P1-N4 and P2-N3) help the storage nodes recover to their initial value after particle strikes and secure robustness under high radiation conditions.

Although Nwise improves fault tolerance, it can suffer from poor cell stability under voltage scaling [8]. This is a common problem also for the other radiation-hardened cells presented in the previous section. To overcome the stability problem, a

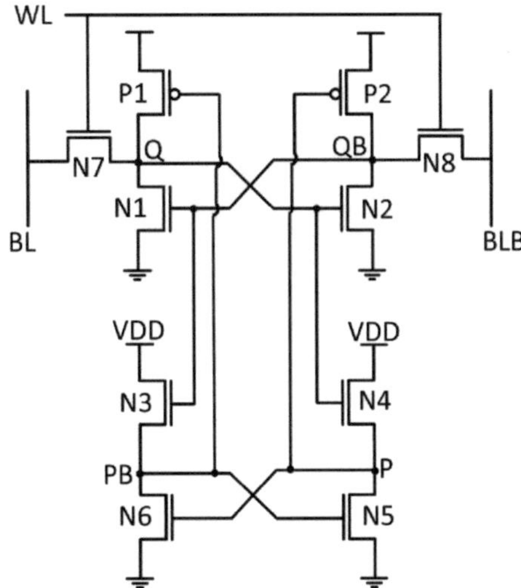

Figure 1.
Circuit details of the Nwise cell.

single-ended read port SRAM cell is proposed in [26], which can separate the read bit line from the storage node with the help of two added NMOS transistors. In this way, the stability of the SRAM cell is improved during read operation, which allows further scaling toward threshold levels [8]. Inspired by this technique, our Adapted Nwise cell is chosen for our simulation in this chapter.

We show the structure of the Adapted Nwise cell in **Figure 2**. The main storage part is still the same as the Nwise cell. However, the access paths are separated: N7 and N8 are write access transistors that connect the main storage nodes to the write bit lines (BLW and BLBW). When the write word line (WWL) is high, N7 and N8 are ON, and a write operation is performed. N9 and N10 connect the storage node QB to the read bit line (BLR). During a read operation, read word line (RWL) is high and turns on N10.

2.2 Operation analysis

Figure 3 shows the test bench circuit used in our simulations, which consists of a one-column set containing 64 Adapted Nwise cells and associated peripheral circuitry (read and write precharge circuits and appropriate circuits for read [7] and write operations [27, 28]).

Transistors P3, P4, and P5 keep BLW and BLBW precharged to VDD before the write operation begins. Signals EnableW is set to VDD, hence Data and DataB can be transferred to BLW and BLBW. Signal WWL is set to VDD, the write operation starts, and data can be written to the storage nodes. Before starting the read operation, transistor P6 keeps BLR precharged to VDD. The read operation begins when RWL becomes high, hence BLR is connected to the internal storage node through N9 and N10. When the read data is on BLR, EnableR becomes high, and the NAND gate routes the data to out.

We use 45 nm technology to design the Adapted Nwise cell. The simulations are done with LTspice [29] at different voltage levels (1 to 0.5 V). **Figure 4** shows the transient simulation results of an Adapted Nwise cell located in the test bench column set for a sequence of "Write 1, Read 1, Write 0, and Read 0" operations. It confirms that the write and read operations are completed successfully.

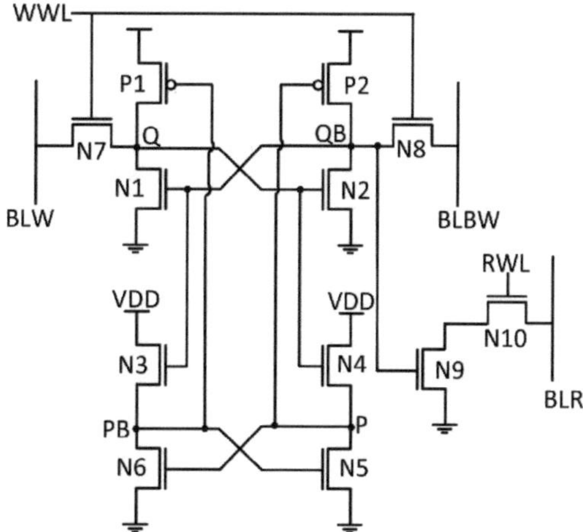

Figure 2.
Circuit details of the adapted Nwise cell.

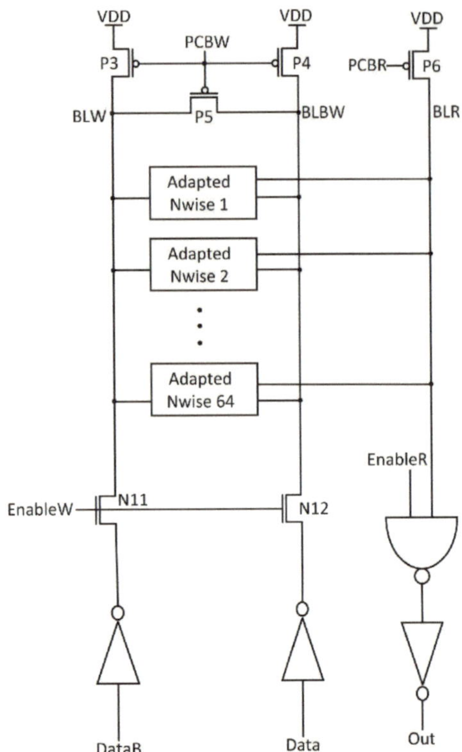

Figure 3.
The test bench circuit consists of a one-column set containing 64 adapted Nwise cells and appropriate circuits for read and write operations [7, 27, 28].

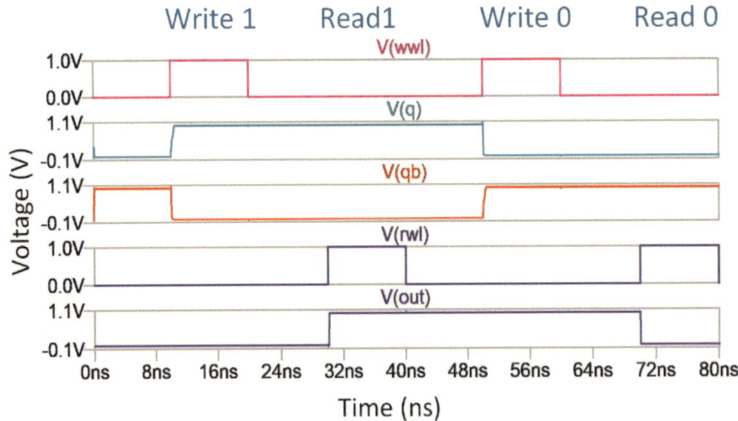

Figure 4.
The simulation waveform of the adapted Nwise cell for a sequential set of operations, write 1, read 1, write 0, and read 0.

2.3 SEU recovery analysis

The SEU robustness of the proposed cell for VDD = 0.5 V is depicted in **Figure 5**. When an energetic particle passes through a semiconductor device, electron-hole

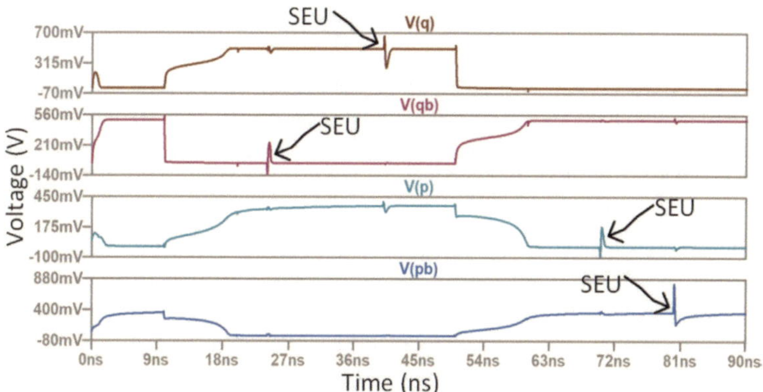

Figure 5.
SEU tolerance simulation of the adapted Nwise cell for VDD = 0.5 V.

pairs are created in its path because it loses its energy [30, 31]. If such an energetic particle strikes a reverse-biased junction depletion region, the injected charge is transported by drift current, leading to an accumulation of extra charge at the node [31]. It produces a transient current pulse that changes the value of the node when the injected charge exceeds the critical charge collected in the node (Q_{crit}) [30, 31]. Hence, sensitive cell nodes are the nodes surrounded by the reverse-biased drain junction of transistor(s) biased in the OFF state [32]. Thus, when a radiation particle strikes a PMOS transistor, only a positive transient pulse ($1 \rightarrow 1$ or $0 \rightarrow 1$) is generated, whereas when a radiation particle strikes an NMOS transistor, only a negative transient pulse ($0 \rightarrow 0$ or $1 \rightarrow 0$) is induced [32]. Let us assume that the Adapted Nwise cell is in state 1 (Q = 1, QB = 0, PB = 0, and P = 1). Therefore, transistors N2, N4, N6, and P1 are ON, and the rest are OFF. Hence, Q, QB, and P are sensitive nodes, while PB is not sensitive to the particle strike.

As shown in **Figure 5**, fault injections that may result in SEUs occur at 25, 40, 70, and 80 ns, respectively. At 25 ns, QB is affected by a particle strike (QB: $0 \rightarrow 1$). We observe that QB returns to its initial state, and followed by it, other nodes return to their initial state. At 40 ns, node Q is affected by a particle strike (Q: $1 \rightarrow 0$). Again, the internal nodes of the Adapted Nwise cell recover their initial state after the injected fault. At 70 ns, P is affected by a particle strike (P: $0 \rightarrow 1$). As can be seen, node P comes back to its initial state, and followed by it, other internal nodes recover their initial state after the injected faults. Finally, PB is affected by a particle strike at 80 ns (PB: $1 \rightarrow 0$). PB also returns to its initial state, and followed by it, other nodes return to their initial state. Hence, the cell is robust against SEUs on all nodes.

The core cell is the same as the Nwise cell. Since the SEU robustness simulations are done in the hold mode, the description of the SEU robustness of the Adapted Nwise cell is the same as that of the Nwise cell [11, 13]. Due to lack of space, we briefly mention the relevant explanations in this article and refer the readers to [11, 13]. In our simulations, we inject charges at cell nodes using the model outlined in Section 2.4. A charge just below the Q_{crit} of the given node is injected to show how this affects the node voltage, and how the SRAM cell recovers its original state. If a charge equal to or greater than Q_{crit} is injected, the SRAM cell would not be able to recover, and a actual SEU would occur.

2.4 Design methodology and simulation results

As mentioned, we design and simulate a one-column set consisting of 64 Adapted Nwise cells and associated peripheral circuitry. The high-level structure is a column in a cache memory as described in [33, 34]. Necessary wire capacitances are added to the bitlines (BLW, BLBW, and BLR) and the wordlines (WWL and RWL) based on the sizes reported in [12, 31, 35].

Transistor sizes of the memory cells, as well as the peripheral circuitry, are optimized to get the maximum robustness, as well as minimum read/write power consumption, minimum read/write access times, and minimum area. However, when the optimization goals are conflicting, more weight is given to robustness. Transistor sizes are chosen for the worst case (VDD = 0.5 V): $W_{P1} = W_{P2} = 60nm, W_{N1} = W_{N2} = 240nm, W_{N3} = W_{N4} = 240nm, W_{N5} = W_{N6} = 60nm, W_{N7} = W_{N8} = 180nm, W_{N9} = W_{N10} = 180nm$.

We use standard manual optimization, tuning transistor sizes to find a global optimized solution. The simulations are performed with LTspice at different voltage levels (1 to 0.5 V) and at a temperature of 27°C. The circuits are designed with a 45 nm predictive technology model. From the simulations, we find the read and write power consumption, read and write access times, and Q_{crit} for different voltage levels.

To simulate the effects of a particle strike injection in a cell node, we use the same model as used in [13]. It is a double exponential current model presented in Eq. (1) that has been widely used by researchers [12, 36, 37]. Q_{dep} is the total charge deposited at the node hit by the particle strike. τ_r is the collection time constant of the junction and τ_f is the ion-track establishing time constant. Both are material-dependent time constants [36]. According to Yassin et al. [38], we set $\tau_r = 164\text{ps}$ and $\tau_f = 50\text{ps}$. We gradually increase Q_{dep} in Eq. (1) in the simulations until the data value stored in the SRAM cell changes and cannot be recovered. This is the critical charge of a given node in an SRAM cell. The cell Q_{crit} is the minimum Q_{crit} among all sensitive nodes of the cell.

$$I(t) = \frac{Q_{dep}}{\tau_f - \tau_r}\left(e^{\frac{-t}{\tau_f}} - e^{\frac{-t}{\tau_r}}\right) \tag{1}$$

Table 1 shows simulation results with the full performance comparison of the Adapted Nwise cell during voltage scaling. The comparisons include power consumption during read and write operations, read access times, write access times, and Q_{crit}.

Supply Voltage Level	Write Power (uW)	Read Power (uW)	Write Access Time (ps)	Read Access Time (ps)	Q_{crit} (fF)
1 V	19.19	8.49	53.16	29.51	101.5
0.9 V	16.61	4.93	63.48	35.31	86.6
0.8 V	15.85	3.06	78.67	43.39	70.7
0.7 V	16.26	2.02	111.48	59.49	51.3
0.6 V	14.67	1.58	176.72	95.74	31.9
0.5 V	9.93	1.10	400.95	196.48	15.9

Table 1.
Cost comparison for the adapted Nwise cell for different supply voltage levels.

3. System-scenario-based design methodology

As we mentioned in Section 1, the system-scenario-based design methodology is a combined design-time and run-time methodology [39] to exploit the application's dynamic behavior at run time, leading to significant optimization potential. According to our simulations, the energy consumption is reduced by combining voltage scaling techniques applied to SRAM cells with the system-scenario-based design method in our framework. A two-phase design-time/run-time system scenario design methodology is detailed in [24]. Here, we describe the methodology according to our use case:

3.1 Case study: space weather forecast

The main idea is to adapt the supply voltage according to the probability of SEUs. When the probability is high, we increase the supply voltage to make the memory more robust against radiation. On the other hand, we reduce the supply voltage to save power when the probability for SEUs is low.

In space, a satellite is exposed to different doses of radiation, depending on, for example, the solar activity. Various agencies provide forecasts for the space weather, that is. the electron or proton flux, based on solar activity. As a case study, we choose the available online information for historic solar weather from [40]. We extract proton flux numbers from November 2004 to May 2022 from the graph. The graph shows samples of the average solar flux units per month, and we choose this parameter as a knob to select the appropriate scenario. In this case, the granularity is relatively coarse, and the power supply voltage can only be adjusted once a month. This is historically coarse-grained statistics. An operational system would have to be based on space weather predictions that typically are valid for a 3 day period, with a forecasted granularity of down to three-hour windows, in which the VDD can be adjusted to the predicted case for each window. **Table 2** shows the number of samples in each range of solar flux.

A correlation between the solar flux level and the probability of SEU has been reported in [41]. We also assume that the energy of the particles reaching the chip surface is sufficiently moderated by passing through metallic shielding [42]. Under these realistic assumptions, we observe flux levels between 5 and 160 MeV. At design time, we identify run-time situations (RTSs) and cluster them into six scenarios:

Range of flux level	Number of one-month samples in each range
0–45 MeV	0
45 MeV – 60 MeV	0
60 MeV – 85 MeV	115
85 MeV – 110 MeV	47
110 MeV – 130 MeV	32
130 MeV – 160 MeV	17

Table 2.
Number of samples at each range of solar flux [40].

1. The first scenario is defined for flux levels below 45 MeV. For this situation, we choose VDD = 0.5 V. The system is in low-power consumption mode, but at the cost of lowest fault tolerance.

2. The second scenario is defined for flux levels between 45 and 60 MeV (45 MeV $< \text{flux} \leq 60\text{MeV}$). For this situation, we choose VDD = 0.6 V.

3. The third scenario is defined for flux levels between 60 and 85 MeV (60 MeV < flux $\leq 85\text{MeV}$). For this situation, we choose VDD = 0.7 V.

4. The fourth scenario is defined for flux levels between 85 and 110 MeV (85 MeV $< \text{flux} \leq 110\text{MeV}$). For this situation, we choose VDD = 0.8 V.

5. The fifth scenario is defined for flux levels between 110 and 130 MeV (110 MeV $< \text{flux} \leq 130\text{MeV}$). For this situation, we choose VDD = 0.9 V.

6. The sixth scenario is defined for flux levels between 130 and 160 MeV (130 MeV $< \text{flux} \leq 160\text{MeV}$). For this situation, we choose VDD = 1 V. The system has the highest level of fault tolerance but at the cost of high power consumption.

At run time, the satellite is informed from Earth when the solar activity changes, and scenarios are dynamically selected accordingly. We now calculate the total power consumption in two cases: (a) when the system scenario method is applied and the system can run at different voltage levels, and (b) when the system runs only at a fixed nominal voltage level.

To calculate power consumption, we need the following information: **Table 1**, which shows cost comparison for the Adapted Nwise cell for different supply voltage levels. **Table 2**, which shows the number of samples in each solar flux range. Furthermore, the number of each level-one cache operation, which is available for a tested benchmark [43]. According to Petersen [43], the number of read and write operations for a tested application of the STAMP benchmark suite, Genome, are as follows: 400449 and 25,028.

We calculate the total power consumption of the first case as follows: (1) The total power consumption for each voltage level is calculated according to the information obtained from **Table 1**, and the number of each operation reported in [43]. (2) The number of samples for each scenario is multiplied by the number of corresponding total power calculated in 1. (3) The results of all scenarios are added together.

For example, we examine the sixth scenario: the number of samples in this range is 17. We choose VDD = 1 V for this scenario. The power consumption for each sample is calculated as follows:

$$Power_{sample} = [(400449 * 8.49uW) + (25028 * 19.19uW)]/(400449 + 25028) \quad (2)$$

Therefore, the total power consumption is obtained by multiplying this number by the number of samples in this range (17), which is equal to 155.03 uW. Similarly, we calculate the total power consumption for each scenario. Then, we add them all together, which results in 842.47 uW.

For the second case: (1) The total power consumption is calculated only for VDD = 1 V according to the information obtained from **Table 1** and the number of each operation reported in [43]. The power consumption for each sample is the same

Cache Designs	Power Consumption (uW)
Original Nwise cache design with a fixed nominal power supply level	1662.93
Adapted Nwise cache design with a fixed nominal power supply level	1924.11
Adapted Nwise cache design with adapted power supply levels according to system scenario design methodology	842.47

Table 3.
The total power consumption of each cache design.

as Eq. (2). (2) The total number of samples (211) is multiplied by the number of power consumption calculated in 1), which is equal to 1924.11 uW.

In this way, we have demonstrated a 56.2% power saving compared to using Adapted Nwise with fixed nominal power supply level. We repeat our simulation for a cache consisting of the original Nwise cell depicted in **Figure 1**. The total power consumption of this cache is calculated as follows:

$$Power_{total} = 211 * (400449 * 7.49uW + 25028 * 14.14uW)/(400449 + 25028) \quad (3)$$

which is equal to 1662.93 uW, 13.6% lower than that of a cache containing of Adapted Nwise cells (at VDD = 1 V). Using the Adapted Nwise cell in combination with system scenario-controlled voltage scaling reduces the power consumption by 49.3% compared to using the original Nwise cell. **Table 3** summarizes the results.

It should be mentioned that we do not consider the loss induced by the circuitry generating the different voltage levels. We assume that this memory will be used in systems, where dynamic voltage and frequency scaling are anyway used for the regular logic.

4. Conclusions and future work

In this chapter, we present a radiation-hardened memory design, which keeps the reliability during voltage scaling. Inspired by the Nwise cell, a recently proposed highly reliable radiation-hardened SRAM cell, we present the design of the Adapted Nwise cell, including calculations of its Q_{crit}, energy consumption, and access time for each operation during voltage scaling. Simulations show that this design can operate at nominal voltage levels down to low-voltage levels for space applications.

In addition, we leverage the scenario-based design methodology to optimize energy consumption at run time and according to our use case: solar activity. Our simulations show that we save up to 49.3% in power consumption compared to using a cache design with a fixed nominal power supply level.

As a future work, an operational system will be made practical by leveraging information from space weather forecasts, thus adjusting the VDD value based on the expected solar flux. Space weather forecasts are given as a three-day prediction and a methodology to extract relevant prediction parameters and distribute them in time to a space system using the Adapted Nwise cell memory must be developed. In addition, process, voltage, and temperature (PVT) variations will be investigated in our future work.

Acknowledgements

This work was funded by the European Union's Horizon 2020 research and innovation program under the Marie Sklodowska-Curie Grant Agreement No. 799481.

The authors thank Gunnar Maehlum and Dirk Meier from the company Integrated Detector Electronics AS (ideas) for their help and fruitful comments that greatly improved the design and experiments.

Author details

Azam Seyedi*, Per Gunnar Kjeldsberg and Roger Birkeland
Faculty of Information Technology and Electrical Engineering, Department of Electronic Systems, Norwegian University of Science and Technology (NTNU), Trondheim, Norway

*Address all correspondence to: azamseyedi2013@gmail.com

References

[1] ARM Developer [Internet]. 2012. Available from: https://developer.arm.com/Processors/Cortex-A53.php [Accessed: October 21, 2022]

[2] Intel Core i3-1215UL Processors [Internet]. Available from: https://www.intel.com/content/www/us/en/products/sku/230902/intel-core-i31215ul-processor-10m-cache-up-to-4-40-ghz/specifications.html [Accessed: October 21, 2022]

[3] Wong W, Koh C, Chen Y, Li H. VOSCH: Voltage scaled cache hierarchies. In: Proceeding of 25th International Conference on Computer Design (ICCD). Lake Tahoe, California, USA: IEEE; 2007. pp. 496-503

[4] Zhang C, Vahid F, Najjar W. A highly configurable cache for low energy embedded systems. ACM Transactions on Embedded Computing Systems. 2005;**4**:363-387

[5] Lin D, Xu Y, Liu X, Zhu W, Dai L, Zhang M, et al. A novel highly reliable and low-power radiation hardened SRAM bit-cell design. IEICE Electronics Express. 2018;**15**(3):20171129

[6] Lin S, Kim Y, Lombardi F. Analysis and design of nanoscale CMOS storage elements for single-event hardening with multiple-node upset. IEEE Transaction on Device Materials Reliability. 2012;**12**(1):68-77

[7] Calhoun BH, Chandrakasan A. A 256kb sub-threshold SRAM in 65 nm CMOS. In: Proceeding of IEEE International Solid State Circuits Conference - Digest of Technical Papers. San Francisco, California, USA: IEEE; 2006. pp. 2592-2601

[8] Verma N, Chandrakasan A. A 256 kb 65 nm 8T subthreshold SRAM employing sense-amplifier redundancy. IEEE Journal of Solid-State Circuits. 2008; **43**(1):141-149

[9] Jahinuzzaman SM, Rennie DJ, Sachdev M. A soft error tolerant 10T SRAM bit-cell with differential read capability. IEEE Transaction on Nuclear Science. 2009;**56**(6):3768-3773

[10] Guo J, Zhu L, Sun Y, Cao H, Huang H, Wang T, et al. Design of area-efficient and highly reliable RHBD 10T memory cell for aerospace applications. IEEE Transactions on Very Large Scale Integration (VLSI) Systems. 2018;**26**(5): 991-994

[11] Seyedi A, Aunet S, Kjeldsberg PG. Nwise and Pwise: 10T radiation hardened SRAM cells for space applications with high reliability requirements. IEEE Access. 2022;**10**: 30624-30642

[12] Jiang J, Xu Y, Zhu W, Xiao J, Zou S. Quadruple cross-coupled latch-based 10T and 12T SRAM bit-cell designs for highly reliable terrestrial applications. IEEE Transactions on Circuits and Systems I: Regular Papers. 2019;**66**(3):967-977

[13] Seyedi A, Aunet S, Kjeldsberg PG. Nwise: An area efficient and highly reliable radiation hardened memory cell designed for space applications. In: Proceeding of IEEE Nordic Circuits and Systems Conference (NORCAS): NORCHIP and International Symposium of System-on-Chip (SoC). Helsinki, Finland: IEEE; 2019. pp. 1-6

[14] Seyedi A, Yalcin G, Unsal O, Cristal A. Circuit design of a novel adaptable and reliable L1 data cache. In: Proceedings of the 23rd ACM International Conference on Great Lakes Symposium on VLSI (GLSVLSI). Paris,

France: Association for Computing Machinery; 2013. pp. 333-334

[15] Yalcin G, Seyedi A, Unsal O, Cristal A. Flexicache: Highly reliable and low- power cache under supply voltage scaling. High Performance Computing. 2014;**1**:173-190

[16] Wilkerson C, Gao H, Alameldeen AR, Chishti Z, Khellah M, Lu S-L. Trading off cache capacity for reliability to enable low voltage operation. In: Proceeding of International Symposium on Computer Architecture (ISCA). Beijing, China: IEEE; 2008. pp. 203-214

[17] Ansari A, Feng S, Gupta S, Mahlke S. Archipelago: A polymorphic cache design for enabling robust near-threshold operation. In: Proceeding of EEE 17th International Symposium on High Performance Computer Architecture. San Antonio, Texas; USA: IEEE; 2011. pp. 539-550

[18] Banaiyan MA, Homayoun H, Dutt N. FFT-cache: A flexible fault-tolerant cache architecture for ultra-low voltage operation. In: Proceeding of 14th International Conference on Compilers, Architectures and Synthesis for Embedded Systems (CASES). Taipei, Taiwan: IEEE; 2011. pp. 95-104

[19] Alameldeen AR, Wagner I, Chishti Z, Wu W, Wilkerson C, Lu S-L. Energy-efficient cache design using variable-strength error-correcting codes. In: Proceeding of 38th Annual International Symposium on Computer Architecture (ISCA). San Jose, CA, USA: IEEE; 2011. pp. 461-471

[20] Chishti Z, Alameldeen AR, Wilkerson C, Wu W, Lu S-L. Improving cache lifetime reliability at ultra-low voltages. In: Proceeding of 42nd Annual IEEE/ACM International Symposium on Microarchitecture (MICRO). New York, NY, USA: IEEE; 2009. pp. 89-99

[21] Qureshi MK, Chishti Z. Operating SECDED-based caches at ultra-low voltage with FLAIR. In: Proceeding of 43rd Annual IEEE/IFIP International Conference on Dependable Systems and Networks (DSN). Budapest, Hungary: IEEE; 2013. pp. 1-11

[22] Carbin M, Misailovic S, Martin C. Verifying quantitative reliability of programs that execute on unreliable hardware. ACM SIGPLAN Notices. 2013; **48**(10):33-52

[23] Filippopoulos I, Catthoor F, Kjeldsberg PG. Exploration of energy efficient memory organisations for dynamic multimedia applications using system scenarios. Design Automation for Embedded Systems. 2013;**17**:669-692

[24] Gheorghita S, Palkovic M, Hamers J, Vandecappelle A, Mamagkakis S, Basten T, et al. System-scenario-based design of dynamic embedded systems. ACM Transactions on Design Automation of Electronic Systems. 2009;**14**(1):1-45

[25] Oleynik Y, Gerndt M, Schuchart J, Kjeldsberg PG, Nagel WE. Run-time exploitation of application dynamism for energy-efficient exascale computing (READEX). In: Proceeding of 18th International Conference on Computational Science and Engineering. Porto, Portugal: IEEE Computer Society; 2015. pp. 347-350

[26] Chang L, Fried DM, Hergenrother J, Sleight JW, Dennard RH, Montoye RK, et al. Stable SRAM cell design for the 32 nm node and beyond. In: Digest of Technical Papers Symposium on VLSI Technology. Kyoto, Japan: IEEE; 2005. pp. 128-129

[27] Maroof N, Kong BS. Charge sharing write driver and half-vdd pre-charge 8t

SRAM with virtual ground for low-power write and read operation. IET Circuits, Devices Systems. 2018;**12**(1):94-98

[28] Jaeyoung K, Pinaki M. A robust 12T SRAM cell with improved write margin for ultra-low power applications in 40nm CMOS. Integration. 2017;**57**: 1-10

[29] [Internet]. Available from: https://www.analog.com/en/design-center/design-tools-and-calculators/ltspice-simulator.html [Accessed: October 21, 2022]

[30] Atias L, Teman A, Giterman R, Meinerzhagen P, Fish A. A low-voltage radiation-hardened 13T SRAM bitcell for ultra-low power space applications. IEEE Transactions on Very Large Scale Integration (VLSI) Systems. 2016;**24**(8): 2622-2633

[31] Guo J, Xiao L, Mao Z. Novel low-power and highly reliable radiation hardened memory cell for 65 nm CMOS technology. IEEE Transactions on Circuits and Systems I: Regular Papers. 2014;**61**(7):1994-2001

[32] Kelin LH, Klas L, Mounaim B, Prasanthi R, Linscott IR, Inan US, et al. LEAP: Layout design through error-aware transistor positioning for soft-error resilient sequential cell design. In: Proceeding of IEEE International Reliability Physics Symposium. Anaheim, CA, USA: IEEE; 2010. pp. 203-212

[33] Seyedi A, Armejach A, Cristal A, Unsal O, Hur I, Valero M. Circuit design of a dual-versioning L1 data cache for optimistic concurrency. In: Proceedings of the 21st Edition of the Great Lakes Symposium on Great Lakes Symposium on VLSI (GLSVLSI). Lausanne, Switzerland: Association for Computing Machinery; 2011. pp. 325-330

[34] Armejach A, Seyedi A, Titos-Gil R, Hur I, Cristal A, Unsal OS, et al. Using a reconfigurable L1 data cache for efficient version management in hardware transactional memory. In: Proceeding of International Conference on Parallel Architectures and Compilation Techniques. Galveston, Texas, USA: IEEE; 2011. pp. 361-371

[35] Guo J, Xiao L, Wang T, Liu S, Wang X, Mao Z. Soft error hardened memory design for nanoscale complementary metal oxide semiconductor technology. IEEE Transactions on Reliability. 2015;**64**(2): 596-602

[36] Messenger GC. Collection of charge on junction nodes from ion tracks. IEEE Transactions on Nuclear Science. 1982; **29**(6):2024-2031

[37] Lin S, Kim Y, Lombardi F. A 11-transistor nanoscale CMOS memory cell for hardening to soft errors. IEEE Transaction on VLSI Systems. 2011; **19**(5):900-904

[38] Qi C, Xiao L, Wang T, Li J, Li L. A highly reliable memory cell design combined with layout-level approach to tolerant single-event upsets. IEEE Transactions on Device and Materials Reliability. 2016;**16**(3):388-395

[39] Yassin Y, Catthoor F, Kjeldsberg PG, Perkis A. Techniques for dynamic hardware management of streaming media applications using a framework for system scenarios. Microprocessors and Microsystems. 2018;**56**:157-168

[40] Space Weather Prediction Center [Internet]. Available from: https://www.swpc.noaa.gov/communities/space-weather-enthusiasts-dashboard [Accessed: 2022-10-21]

[41] The Space Environment Information System [Internet]. Available from: https://www.spenvis.oma.be/help/backg

round/flare/flare.html [Accessed: October 21, 2022]

[42] Petersen E. Single Event Effects in Aerospace. Wiley-IEEE Press; 2011 Online ISBN: 9781118084328. DOI: 10.1002/9781118084328

[43] Seyedi A, Armejach A, Cristal A, Unsal OS, Valero M. Novel SRAM bias control circuits for a low power L1 data cache. In: Proceeding of NORCHIP. Copenhagen, Denmark: IEEE; 2012. pp. 1-6

Chapter 3

A Review on Non-Volatile and Volatile Emerging Memory Technologies

Siddhartha Raman Sundara Raman

Abstract

As technology scaling is approaching a stand-still with architectural advancements on modern day processors struggling to improve performance, coupled with the rise in machine learning topologies demanding better performing processors, there is a pressing need to address the reasons behind today's performance bottleneck. These reasons include long access latency of memory technologies, scalability of memory designs, energy inefficiency incurred by increased performance, and additional area overhead. To explore these issues, a holistic understanding of existing memory technologies is essential. In this chapter, a review of different memory designs starting from volatile memory technologies such as Static Random Access Memory (SRAM), Dynamic Random Access Memory (DRAM), NAND/NOR flash to emerging non-volatile memory technologies such as Resistive Random Access Memory (RRAM), Magneto-resistive random access memory (MRAM), Ferroelectric Field effect transistor (FeFET) is presented, with specific consideration of tradeoffs involving area, performance, energy.

Keywords: memory, SRAM, DRAM, non-volatile memory, NAND/NOR, RRAM, FeFET, MRAM

1. Introduction

Modern day systems typically consist of a central processing unit responsible for performing arithmetic and logical operations on the data stored in memory. This architecture is called the Von-Neumann architecture, wherein there are dedicated logic and arithmetic units inside the CPU and the data is read/written from/into memory, and has been the foundational architecture for high performance CPUs till date. A brief background of these CPUs suggest that these processors have undergone tremendous improvements beginning from in-order CPUs that execute the instructions in program order, to modern-day out-of-order CPUs that execute instructions as soon as they are ready to execute and still give an impression to the software that the instructions were executed in-order. This has resulted in an increased performance, with frequencies ranging as high as GHz. However, the major bottleneck from improving the performance further has been the tremendously low memory performance [1, 2], often referred to as the memory-wall bottleneck. To alleviate this, an in-depth analysis of existing/emerging memory technologies is required to understand the problems in each of the technologies and further propose solutions. Therefore, in this chapter, we give a brief overview on the existing technologies and the solutions proposed in the literature to understand the tradeoffs made between energy, area and performance. The technologies described are (i) Static Random Access Memory (SRAM), (ii) Dynamic Random Access Memory (DRAM), (iii) NAND/NOR flash (iv) Resistive Random Access Memory (RRAM), (v) Magneto-resistive Random Access Memory (MRAM), (vi) Ferroelectric Field effect Transistor (FeFET). The major reason behind choosing these devices as the case study for non-volatile memories is that there has been a tremendous growth in the recent times about potential of replacing the existing memory topologies with these devices, as they offer bitcell density advantage.

2. Memory technologies

The memory technologies can be classified into volatile and non-volatile memory technologies depending on whether the data is retained in memory in the absence of power supply. From an architectural perspective, processors use caches made of SRAM that are responsible for fast memory accesses and main-memory made of DRAM optimized for density/cost. The hard disk/secondary storage are made of non-volatile memory technologies like NAND Flash and are further optimized for higher density/lower cost.

2.1 Volatile memory technology

The major memory technologies that are present in the modern-day computers are made of SRAM, DRAM and embedded DRAM (eDRAM). SRAMs have been the workhorse of high performance caches, as they have low access latencies as compared to other memory technologies. Commodity DRAMs have been used in main memory storage, as they have the advantages of high density and a simple bitcell structure. Embedded DRAMs have started to gain traction for caches as they offer higher performance (than commodity DRAM) and high density with a simple bitcell structure, which will be discussed in detail in this section.

2.1.1 Static random access memory (SRAM)

SRAMs are classified into 6 T, 7 T, 8 T,9 T and 10 T structures [3]. The most commonly used SRAM bitcells are the 6 T and 8 T bitcells. Both these bitcells make use of a cross-coupled inverter as the storage element. The 6 T structure is used when overall SRAM area is constrained with high-performance requirements. However, the 8 T structure is used in high-performance cache designs, wherein there are no density constraints, because they have the advantage of performing read after write in back-to-back cycles [4]. This section elaborates the tradeoffs in both these designs with respect to performance, area and energy.

2.1.1.1 6 T SRAM

This design makes use of a shared read-write port, thereby ensuring that either read/write can be performed in a cycle, therefore making it a 1R(read)W(write) port design. 6 T SRAMs shown in **Figure 1** consists of a cross-coupled inverter with pull-up

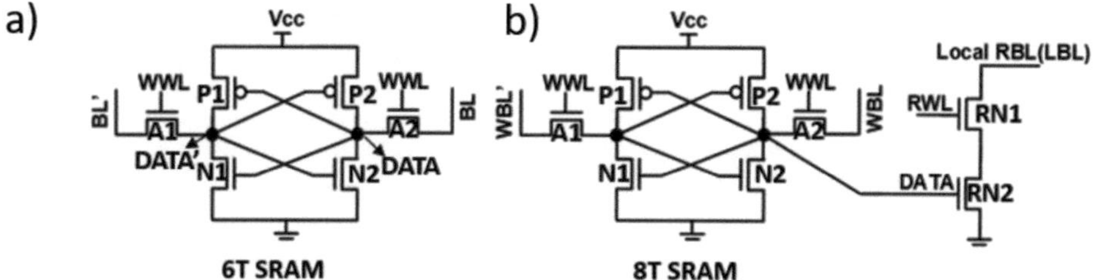

Figure 1.
a) 6 T SRAM, with a shared read/write port, b) 8 T SRAM with decoupled read and write ports.

PMOS transistors named P1, P2 and pull-down NMOS transistors named N1, N2 and the NMOS access transistors named A1, A2. In the case of a write operation, data is written onto the bitcell by conditioning the bit lines (BL) to the data value that needs to be stored in the bitcell [5]. For instance, for writing '1' onto the bitcell, BL is driven high with a voltage of Vcc and BL' is driven low with a voltage of 0. WWL voltage is driven high so that the DATA node holds a value of '1' and DATA' node holds a '0'. This operation can be split further into 2 phases, namely the initiation and completion phase. The initiation of writing '1' onto the DATA node begins by writing '0' onto the DATA' node, as the NMOS access transistor A1 can pass a good '0', as opposed to NMOS access transistor A2 passing a good '1'. Thus, DATA' going low would imply that the PMOS P2 is slowly being turned ON, thus helping A2 to further write a good '1' onto the bitcell, even though A2 does not pass a good '1' during the completion phase. In order to accomplish a good initiation, the access transistor marked A1 should have a high drive strength as compared to PMOS P1 so that BL' is written successfully onto the DATA' node. In the case of writing a '0' onto DATA node, A2 initiates the process and is completed by the PMOS P1 driving DATA node to Vcc [6]. In this case, the design constraint is that the drive strength of A2 must be greater than the drive strength of P2 to accomplish a successful completion. Generalizing this, the initiation is brought about by the node storing '1' and completed by the node storing '0' in the case of a write operation.

The read is preceded by a precharge operation, wherein the BL is precharged to Vcc. During the read operation, with '0' being stored in the bitcell, the BL discharges through A2, with the WWL turned ON and the difference in voltage between BL and BL' is measured using a sense amplifier, that is sensitive to voltage differences as low as 100 mV [7, 8] in the modern-day SRAM design. The sense amplifier is typically realized by another cross-coupled inverter design, that is designed to offer precise outputs even in the presence of process variations, often leading to design complexity/ overhead. The design constraint during the read operation is that the NMOS transistor should be strong enough to hold the DATA node at '0' even though BL attempts to write a '1' through the access transistor A2.

During the retention phase, the WWLs and BLs are turned OFF and data leaks from the node storing '1' [7]. This occurs because of the voltage difference between BL and DATA node, with the possibility of a bit-flip, making SRAMs volatile. One common approach is to drive the WL to slightly negative voltages to reduce the leakage through the access transistor. Furthermore, the bitcell Vcc cannot be reduced to 0 even during retention, as this would lead to corruption of bitcell contents. Therefore, the bitcell Vcc needs to be maintained at a minimum voltage, leading to an increased power consumption of the processor [7]. This voltage limits the minimum operating voltage of the overall processor design and is often referred to as Vmin. The issues with 6 T SRAM design can be summarized as complex design constraints required for read, write, retention operation in 6 T SRAMs, the need for a separate precharge cycle before the read operation.

2.1.1.2 8 T SRAM

In an attempt to relax the design constraints for read operation and to amortize the cost of a precharge cycle by performing another "useful" task simultaneously, 8 T SRAMs were proposed [6]. These have decoupled read/write ports, wherein the access transistors A1 and A2 are used during the write operation and the transistors RN1 and RN2 are used during the read operation, as shown in **Figure 1**. The major advantage of 8 T SRAM is that precharge of RBL attached to the read port can be done in parallel to the write operation done using the access transistors A1, A2. This can be extremely useful in caches, wherein a commonly seen operation is a read followed by write, for which precharge can be overlapped with write, thereby making the read-after-write a 2 cycle operation, as opposed to it being a 3 cycle operation. Furthermore, because the read port transistors are decoupled from write port transistors, the read is independent of the strength of the N2 and A2 transistors, unlike the 6 T SRAM scenario, thereby enabling better design characteristics. The write/retention operation in this scenario is the same as that of 6 T SRAM [9].

The read operation progresses as: (1) RBL is precharged, (2) RWL is turned ON (3) RBL discharge is sensed. Unlike the case of 6 T SRAM, 8 T SRAM involves full swing discharge of RBL during a read operation, therefore enabling realization of the sense amplifier using digital logic gates like a simple 2-input AND gate, with one input being connected to RBL and the other input connected to a reference voltage driven to Vcc. Furthermore, this form of sensing is called single ended sensing as RBL' is not utilized in sensing, unlike the case of 6 T. A design optimization for improving performance is that instead of sharing the RBL across all the rows in a column, RBL that is sensed for read in the case of 8 T SRAM, is shared across only a few rows in the column (indicated as local RBL), although there is still a RBL shared across all rows in the column (called the global RBL). During the precharge operation, "global RBL" is initially precharged to Vcc, which further precharges "local RBL" to Vcc [10]. However, during the read operation, local RBL discharges and the global RBL is used as the reference voltage for the sensing operation. This decoupling of global and local RBL helps in reducing the discharge latency/read time improving the performance further, as there is lesser capacitance to discharge as opposed to having a higher capacitance, when discharging a complete column [11].

2.1.2 Dynamic random access memories (DRAM)

Commodity DRAMs, used as the main memory storage structure, has the advantages of high storage density owing to its small bitcell size. The bitcell is made of 1T1C (1 Transistor, 1 Capacitor) structure (**Figure 2**) [12], with the capacitor used as the storage element. The capacitor is typically a deep trench capacitor, with its capacitance value in the order of 10s of fF, in order to store the charge with minimal leakage. However, it is still a volatile memory because of the discharge from the "leaky capacitor", requiring periodic refreshes to refresh the data that is stored. This bitcell is optimized for cost, but is manufactured separately, integrated with the processor on a separate chip, leading to long latencies for DRAM accesses [13].

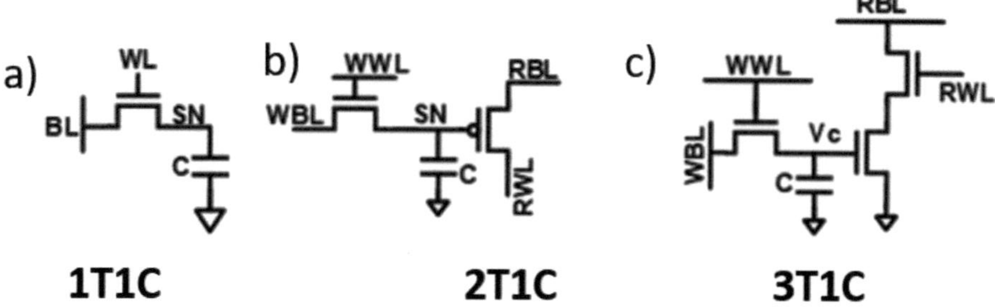

Figure 2.
a) DRAM variants without/ b), c) with decoupled read and write ports with SN/Vc showing the storage node.

2.1.2.1 1T1C

The write operation is accomplished by turning on the WL and driving the BL to the necessary voltage value, thereby charging the bitcell capacitor. The read operation is carried out by first precharging the BL to Vcc/2, turning on WL and using a sense amplifier to sense the voltage drop/increase on the BL [14]. It is important to note that the read operation naturally carries out the refresh operation as the sense amplifier is connected to the BL, therefore driving SN to the sensed value. This refresh action is important because the read of the bitcell is disruptive, as the SN voltage changes during the discharge of BL. For instance, during read of '0', SN settles to a value between 0-Vcc/2 and during read of '1', SN settles to a value between Vcc/2-Vcc. The disadvantage of this design is that the discharge of BL is susceptible to process variations and may lead to inaccurate computations, if the data is not restored/refreshed back by the sense amplifier. During the retention phase, WL is turned off/driven to negative voltages to reduce the leakage through the access transistor.

2.1.2.2 2T1C

Although the commodity DRAMs still make use of 1T1C structure, bitcells have been proposed to eliminate the disruptive read. One such bitcell is 2T1C DRAM (**Figure 2**), that makes use of decoupled read and write ports, These are also called the gain cell DRAM, that make use of WWL and WBL to write a value onto SN and using RBL, RWL to read a value from SN. The write operation is similar to that of 1T1C. Prior to a read operation, the RBL is precharged to '0' in the case of PMOS being the read port transistor. During the read operation of a bitcell storing '0', RWL is turned ON and RBL is charged through the read-port transistor, which is further sensed using a sense amplifier. Similarly, in the case of storing '1', BL does not discharge as the PMOS read port transistor is OFF. However, the major disadvantage with this design is that the available margin for sensing the RBL voltage is limited during a read operation. This can be explained as: Assume there are 'm' rows in a single column that share the same RBL, with RWL corresponding to the unselected/selected rows in a column driven low/high and are storing a '0'/'1'. In such a scenario, RBL charges towards Vcc, because the selected row's WL is turned ON. However, as RBL is ramping up towards the threshold voltage of the read port transistor, the unselected rows experience a path towards gnd through the read port transistor, thereby discharging the RBL differential that was developed and constraining the sense margin to be equal to the threshold voltage of the read port transistor making it susceptible to process variations. In the case of NMOS being used as read port transistor, RBL is precharged to Vcc and the selected/unselected row's RWL driven high/low. In this case, the RBL voltage saturates at Vcc-Vt because of the leakage from the unselected rows, with Vt being the threshold voltage of the NMOS read port transistor [15].

2.1.2.3 3T1C

Although 2T1C offers non-disruptive read mechanism, there was a need to improve the design in terms of resilience to process variations with increased sense margin. To accomplish this, 3T1C structure was proposed with 2 read port transistors (NMOS transistors) and 1 write port NMOS transistor, as seen in **Figure 2**, similar to that of 8 T SRAM. In this case, the write operation is similar to 1T1C design and the read operation is preceded by precharge operation, with RBL precharged to 'Vcc'. During a read operation, RWL is turned ON and RBL starts to discharge, with the additional transistor enabling read-out with higher sense margin by not allowing the unselected rows to discharge the RBL further, unlike 2T1C. This is accomplished by driving RWL of unselected rows to '0', ensuring that the RBL does not discharge through the unselected rows. However, both the 2T1C and 3T1C bitcells need separate refresh cycles, leading to increased power/energy, as the read operation does not imply a refresh operation because of the presence of a separate write and read bit lines (unlike the case of 1T1C) [16].

The major issues with the DRAM are the long access latencies, reduced number of metal layers for routing the DRAM wires, thereby limiting the bandwidth of the memory array [17]. To improve the performance of the DRAM design, embedded DRAMs that have the advantage of monolithic integration with the logic transistors were proposed, Furthermore, these have the advantage of stacking multiple layers and eDRAMs can be stacked in a 3D fashion, allowing increased bandwidth as compared to DRAMs, thereby enabling them to be used in last level caches. These can be designed in similar variants like 1T1C, 2T1C and 3T1C eDRAMs. However, the major disadvantage is that the eDRAMs use back end of the line (metal layers) based bitcell capacitor and scaling the capacitance to higher values is extremely difficult, thereby degrading the retention time of Silicon-based eDRAMs. Therefore, these offer the advantage of improved performance at the cost of lesser retention time. To further improve the retention time and reduce the leakage of eDRAMs, few novel materials based devices like Indium Gallium Zinc Oxide eDRAMs have been proposed, which have extreme low leakage with moderate ON currents have been proposed [18, 19].

2.2 Non-volatile memory technology

Non-volatile memories are important for storing large amount of data that need to be saved for years together, as they retain data even in the absence of voltage supply. These are used extensively in hard disk/solid state drives (SSD) in the modern processors. The technology used in the SSDs is the NAND/NOR flash memory technology, as they have the advantage of easy integration, highly dense bitcell structure, stackable across 3D layers with minimal design effort, low cost/bit technology. This was a major replacement to old-age magnetic memory technology such as floppy, hard disk drives(HDD), which incur extremely long latency operations. The performance of NAND/NOR flash memories is better than the HDD, but worse than the already discussed SRAM/DRAM technology. This section begins by discussing the tradeoffs in the flash memory technologies and further extends to emerging non-volatile memory technologies including Resistive Random Access Memory, Magnetic Random Access Memory.

2.2.1 Flash memory

2.2.1.1 NAND/NOR flash

NAND flash gets its name from the fact that the transistors are connected serially, similar to the pull-down transistors present in a CMOS NAND configuration. NAND has higher density, requires high write voltage, offers high write performance, low read performance as compared to NOR flash. The write operation is classified into programming (writing a '0') and erasing (writing a '1') by modulating the threshold voltage of the transistor that is being written into [20]. The NAND flash technology makes use of a floating and a separate control gate (CG), marked as 2 lines in **Figure 3** transistor as the storage element, with CG trapping the electrons onto the floating gate using Fowler-Nordheim tunneling. In the case of programming, a high voltage is applied on the control gate and this allows the electrons in the channel between source to drain to get attracted onto the floating gate of the transistor, thereby depleting the channel of electrons, effectively increasing the threshold voltage of the transistor, resulting in a storage of '0' [22]. In the case of storing a '1', the electrons that were trapped during the program phase are released by driving the control gate with a negative or 0 voltage. This results in the channel receiving more electrons, thereby decreasing the threshold voltage of the transistor. In the case of NAND flash, there are header and footer transistors that are used during the write and read operations [22].

During the write operation (program), the BL is driven to '0'(0 V), WL corresponding to the selected row is driven high (for instance, ~20 V), with the other rows in the column driven with a voltage sufficient to pass the BL voltage onto the source of the row of transistors that are being written into and the gate to source voltage for selected cell is high to ensure that the tunneling happens. Furthermore, the header device is turned ON (for instance, ~4 V) to ensure that the BL voltage is passed onto the selected row. On the unselected columns, the BL is driven high (for instance, ~4 V), and as the NMOS transistors are not good at passing '1'(for instance, ~4 V), the header transistor goes into sub-threshold region, (as the drain = Vcc, source = Vcc-Vt, gate being at Vt). Thus, shutting down of the header transistor enables a non-disruptive operation on the unselected columns. In the case of

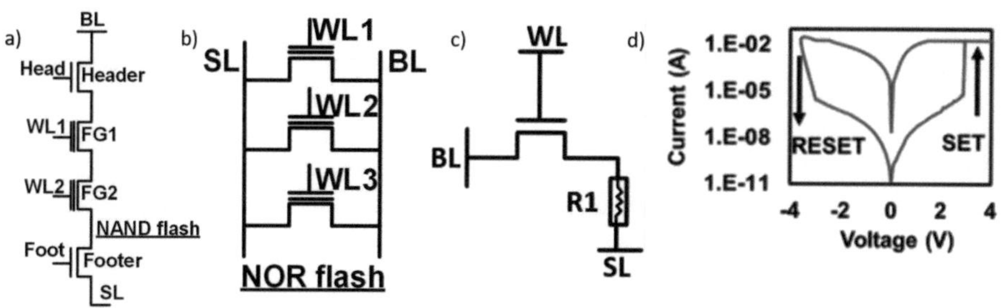

Figure 3.
a) NAND and b) NOR flash, c) RRAM bitcell (1T1R) d) RRAM I-V characteristics [21].

programming, similar to other memory technologies, only a row is programmed, whereas in the case of erasing, a block of memory is erased. In other words, a memory array completely is erased [23].

During the erasing scenario, BL is initialized to 0 to ensure that all intermediate source and drain voltages are at 0 and are then left floating. SL can be left floating and the WL of the floating gate transistors are kept at 0 to ensure that the trapped electrons are ejected out of the floating gate into the channel for an entire memory array of cells. The header and footer word lines are turned ON, thereby ensuring that the source/drain voltages are 0 [24].

In the case of reading from NAND flash, the read is similar to programming in that the granularity of read is still a row of bitcells, unlike the case of erasing. The read of NAND flash can be accomplished by turning on the WLs of unselected rows to pass voltage, with BL driven high and SL driven low. The gate of the selected row is driven low and the current at the BL is measured across all columns to identify the read value from a row of cells. Furthermore, the major reason for NAND flash being used extensively for SSDs is the possibility of storing multiple levels in a bit-cell. There have been proposals suggesting storage of as high as, 1024 levels in a single bitcell. However, the major disadvantage of the flash technology is the voltages needed for operation can be extremely high in the order of 20 V for programming, to capture electrons into the floating gate, limiting the power on the design and thereby it suffers from thermal bottleneck issues. The future of this technology lies in the ability to stack multiple layers with minimal coupling coefficient between layers. From a point of view of NOR flash, it is used only in microcontroller/internet of things based application space in older technology nodes and is still premature when it comes to usage in advanced technology, with a density as high as NAND flash [25].

2.2.2 Resistive random access memory (RRAM)

These are a class of emerging memory technology that rely on the principle of distinguishing the memory contents on the basis of resistance of the bitcell. The idea of using resistance based memory is helped by the fact that a variety of oxides exhibit resistive switching, i.e. the resistance changes as a function of the voltage applied between them (like HfO_2, TiO_2) and these binary metal oxides are easily compatible with CMOS [26]. There are different RRAM variants like that of conductive bridge RRAM and oxide RRAM (detailed in this section). The conductive bridge RRAM (also known as electrochemical metallization memory) makes use of a metal ion for the formation of filament and rely on the movement of metal ions to determine the resistance of the device and subsequent switching. The oxide RRAM bitcell consists of metal (top electrode)-insulator-metal (bottom electrode) (R1 marked in **Figure 3**), with the insulator being the above-mentioned oxides and rely on formation or breaking of oxide filament to store '1'(set) and '0'(reset), with Joule heating predicted to be the reason for filament rupture [27]. There are 2 types of RRAM namely the unipolar and bipolar RRAM, distinguished on the basis of voltages necessary to perform switching. It is important to understand the device characteristics to understand the applications and tradeoffs of the bitcell. In the case of bipolar switching, which is the most common usage of RRAM, the switching would involve applying positive voltages between the top and bottom electrode to perform "set operation" and applying negative voltages between the top and bottom electrode to perform the "reset operation". In the case of unipolar RRAM based switching mechanism, only positive voltage is sufficient to undergo set-reset and reset-set changes. **Figure 3** describes the I-V characteristics for a bipolar switching RRAM, wherein the set voltage is high in the range of for instance, 3–3.2 V and the reset voltage is in the range of -ve for instance, 3–3.2 V [21]. The set and reset voltages need not be in the similar range and the set voltage can be considerably higher than the reset voltage, depending on the oxide insulator between the two electrodes. However, there are other devices of RRAM that have been proposed in the literature to reduce RRAM set/reset voltage to as low as for instance, 1 V [21]. With the initial state of the RRAM assumed to be in reset, the voltage is increased from 0 to the voltage necessary for setting, forming the filament necessary for conduction across RRAM, thereby allowing a low resistance path between the top and the bottom electrodes, shown as the set operation. Increasing the voltage beyond the set voltage strengthens the filament formation, and does not increase the current, marked by the saturation of current. In devices, wherein the current keeps increasing, a compliance current is maintained to restrict the increasing current to a certain threshold. In the case of decreasing the voltage from beyond set voltages towards 0, the current keeps decreasing, with a voltage of 0 still holding the filament, thereby having a non-zero current when the voltage comes back to 0. On decreasing the voltage in the negative directions, the current initially starts increasing till the voltage becomes equal to the reset voltage. On reaching the reset voltage, the current saturates and programs it into reset mode (that is, the filament formation is broken). Once the reset voltage is achieved, decreasing the voltage below the reset voltage breaks down the filament, thereby decreasing the current flowing through and increasing the resistance between the electrodes. These are non-volatile memory because the filament does not break/form if the current state is an already formed/ broken filament, even when left without supplying voltage to retain the contents of the bitcell [6, 21].

It is important to understand the memory topology that is present to obtain a bitcell that can be used for storing. Similar to commodity DRAM structure, the RRAM based memory makes use of 1T1R structure wherein the access transistor has a WL that is responsible for accessing the bitcell. In the case of setting RRAM (storing '1'), a high voltage is applied on the BL node with SL node closer to 0, so that there is enough differential across the RRAM to obtain the filament, with WL turned ON. In the case of resetting RRAM (storing '0'), a high voltage is applied on the SL node with BL node closer to 0, breaking the filament formed by the set process. The design constraint in the case of setting is that the voltage at WL needs to be high enough to allow a high voltage through the access transistor, as NMOS based access transistors are not good at allowing '1' and saturates at Vcc-Vt. This should be taken into account when identifying the right BL voltage for setting. During the reset process, driving BL with a negative voltage is not preferred as the unselected rows in the same column would have WL equal to 0 and having a high negative voltage on the BL would mean a high negative voltage between the gate and the source of unselected rows, causing Gate Induced Drain Leakage (GIDL). Hence, SL is driven with a positive value, making sure that the difference between voltage at the top and bottom node is negative, thereby resetting the filament formation. In the case of read, the voltage at RBL is driven to a predefined value and based on the amount of current flowing through the bitcell, the contents of the bitcell are identified. In the case of set mode, since the RRAM is in a lower resistance state, the amount of current sensed on the BL would be higher, indicating '1' and in the case of reset mode, since the RRAM is in a higher resistance state, the amount of current would be low, indicating '0' [28]. During a read operation, the constraint is that the read voltage should not be high enough to alter the state of the bitcell and just a "disturb voltage" is sufficient to accomplish a successful read. The ratio of high resistance state's resistance to low resistance state's resistance determines read margin of RRAM. In the case of RRAMs having high ratio of OFF to ON resistance, read margin is high and is resilient to process variations. Similar to the NAND flash, RRAM can be used effectively to store multiple levels in a single bitcell thereby adding to the advantage of dense bitcell. The disadvantages of RRAM involve the higher set/reset voltages, high read/write latency and lower endurance ($\sim 10^6$ cycles) as compared to the conventional SRAM/DRAM technology.

2.3 Magneto-resistive random access memory (MRAM)

MRAM, like the RRAM also belongs to a class of memory technology that relies on the resistance of different states to store different contents onto the bitcell and builds concepts from magnetism/Spin Hall effect to modulate the bitcell resistance, hence the name magneto-resistive memory [29]. There are different types of MRAM namely the spin transfer torque (STT MRAM), Spin orbit torque MRAM (SOT MRAM) distinguished on the basis of the mechanism used for writing into the bitcell. The advantage of the bitcell as compared to RRAM is that the endurance of the bitcell is extremely high (in the order of $\sim 10^{15}$ cycles) with the write voltage slightly lower and lower write latency as compared to RRAM [30]. However, the disadvantage of this device lies in the complexity of integrating the different parts of the device together and the ratio of OFF to ON resistance is lower as compared to RRAM. However, the complexity of fabrication of the device has been taken care of, as STT MRAMs (**Figure 4**) are ready for mass production. The magnetic tunnel junction (MTJ) which is the primary storage element for STT-MRAM, consists of 3 layers namely pinned, spacer layer and free layer with the relative orientation between the pinned and free layer determining the magneto-resistance of the device. The pinned layer has the magnetic moment pointed in one direction and does not change with application of external voltage. On the contrary, free layer's magnetic moment can be changed with the application of external voltage. If the magnetic moment of pinned layer and free layer point in the same direction, the magneto-resistance is low, and the resistance is high, when the magnetic moments point in the opposite direction. Similar to the case of RRAM, the direction of current determines the switching of MRAM and the current flow from pinned layer to free layer is responsible for switching the free layer from parallel (Low resistance - '1') to antiparallel (High resistance - '0') state. The current flow from free layer to pinned layer is responsible for switching from

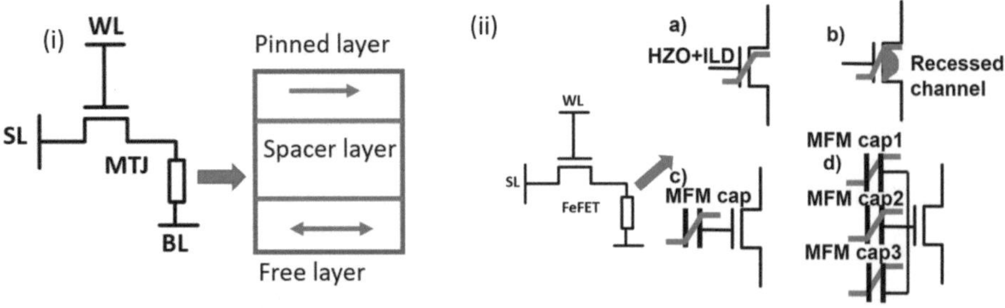

Figure 4.
(i)STT-MRAM and (ii) FeFET bitcell.

antiparallel to parallel state. A read operation is accomplished by applying a voltage at the BL and SL and the current through the MTJ (through single-ended sensing) is an indication of the magneto-resistance of the device [31, 32].

2.4 Ferroelectric field effect transistor (FeFET)

It belongs to a class of technology that makes use of capacitor to store data, similar to DRAM. It is a promising non-volatile memory (NVM) technology as it is dense, similar to RRAM, offers high speed as compared to RRAM and ease of manufacturing as they are compatible with mature CMOS technology nodes. The disadvantages of the existing design include the high program/erase voltage as compared to other NVM designs (order of 4 V) and the lower retention time because of the innate depolarizing field in these devices [33]. FeFETs were formerly realized using a ferroelectric HZO (Hafnium Zinc Oxide) that is sandwiched between the metal and the typical oxide dielectric, as in the case of MOSFET, with the voltage division between the HZO capacitor and dielectric oxide (interlayer dielectric - ILD) for the voltage applied at the gate determining the bitcell content as shown in **Figure 4a**. The major disadvantage is that the voltage drop across dielectric oxide is high and the voltage drop across HZO is minimal, thereby increasing the voltage needed for performing the write operation. Furthermore, there are innate fabrication difficulties to introduce the HZO layer between the gate and interlayer dielectric. To overcome the higher write voltage for FeFET, recessed FeFET was proposed, which increases the voltage drop across HZO, by making a geometry of the source-drain channel to be circular, concentrating the incoming electric field to a smaller region of area. FeMFET tries to overcome the integration difficulties faced by recessed FeFET, by integrating ferroelectric capacitor separately/independently at the gate (**Figure 4b**). This allows optimization of ferroelectric capacitor separately from that of MOSFET and write voltage can be reduced by decreasing the aspect ratio between ferroelectric capacitor and the interlayer dielectric of MOSFET (**Figure 4c**). However, the disadvantage of the design is that it introduces a floating node in between HZO capacitor and interlayer dielectric capacitance that is susceptible to noise, process variations and can reduce the retention time as the depolarizing field increases [34]. Furthermore, it also affects the read voltage considerably, if there is leakage from the unselected cells in the same column. Furthermore, multiple ferroelectric capacitors can be connected in parallel at the gate to make sure that write voltage can be reduced because of the increase in capacitance of the ferroelectric capacitor, thereby making sure that most of the voltage drop is across the ferroelectric capacitor and not across the MOSFET. However, this approach is not scalable to larger voltage ranges and requires 3 cycles for a write operation. The write operation in these bitcells are accomplished by applying a voltage at the gate, and the voltage across the ferroelectric capacitor is an indication of the bitcell content. In the case of read, a read disturb voltage is applied on the top terminal of the ferroelectric capacitor, causing a voltage division, thereby enabling a higher voltage at the gate of the MOSFET, thereby implying a higher current through the FET which would imply '1' and '0' if the current through the MOSFET is lower [35–37].

3. Conclusion

In this chapter, we discussed the different memory technologies starting from volatile memories like Static Random Access Memory (SRAM), Dynamic Random Access

Memory (DRAM) to non-volatile memories like NAND/NOR flash, resistive random access memories (RRAM), magneto-resistive random access memories (MRAM), ferro-electric field effect transistor (FeFET) with specific reference to write, read and retention operations in each of these designs and the design constraints associated with them.

Acknowledgements

I would like to acknowledge Kavya for providing valuable feedback in writing this chapter.

Author details

Siddhartha Raman Sundara Raman
The University of Texas, Austin, USA

*Address all correspondence to: s.siddhartharaman@utexas.edu

References

[1] Raman SRS, Wen F, Pillarisetty R, De V, Kulkarni JP. High noise margin, digital logic design using Josephson junction field-effect transistors for cryogenic computing. IEEE Transactions on Applied Superconductivity. 2021, Art no. 1800105;**31**(5):1-5. DOI: 10.1109/TASC.2021.3054347

[2] Pedram A, Richardson S, Horowitz M, Galal S, Kvatinsky S. Dark memory and accelerator-rich system optimization in the dark silicon era. IEEE Design Test. 2016;**34**(2):39-50

[3] Kulkarni JP, Roy K. Ultralow-Voltage Process-Variation-Tolerant Schmitt-Trigger-Based SRAM Design. IEEE Transactions on Very Large Scale Integration (VLSI) Systems. 2012;**20**(2): 319-332. DOI: 10.1109/TVLSI.2010.2100834

[4] Kim CH et al. A forward body-biased low-leakage SRAM cache: Device, circuit and architecture considerations. IEEE Transactions on Very Large Scale Integration (VLSI) Systems. 2005;**13**(3): 349-357

[5] Pavlov A, Sachdev M. CMOS SRAM Circuit Design and Parametric Test in Nano-Scaled Technologies: Process-Aware SRAM Design and Test. Vol. 40. Springer Science Business Media; 2008

[6] Sundara Raman SR, Nibhanupudi SST, Kulkarni JP. Enabling In-memory computations in non-volatile SRAM designs, in IEEE Journal on Emerging and Selected Topics in Circuits and Systems. 2022;**12**(2):557-568. DOI: 10.1109/JETCAS.2022.3174148

[7] Nibhanupudi SST, Raman SRS, Kulkarni JP. Phase transition material-assisted low-power SRAM design, in IEEE Transactions on Electron Devices. May 2021;**68**(5):2281-2288. DOI: 10.1109/TED.2021.3067849

[8] Wicht B, Nirschl T, Schmitt-Landsiedel D. Yield and speed optimization of a latch-type voltage sense amplifier. IEEE Journal of Solid-State Circuits. 2004;**39**(7): 1148-1158

[9] Morita Y et al. An area-conscious low-voltage-oriented 8T-SRAM design under DVS environment. In: 2007 IEEE Symposium on VLSI Circuits. IEEE; 2007

[10] Verma N, Chandrakasan AP. A 65nm 8T sub-Vt SRAM employing sense-amplifier redundancy. In: 2007 IEEE International Solid-State Circuits Conference. Digest of Technical Papers. IEEE; 2007

[11] Chang L et al. An 8T-SRAM for variability tolerance and low-voltage operation in high-performance caches. IEEE Journal of Solid-State Circuits. 2008;**43**(4):956-963

[12] Farmahini-Farahani A et al. NDA: Near-DRAM acceleration architecture leveraging commodity DRAM devices and standard memory modules. In: 2015 IEEE 21st International Symposium on High Performance Computer Architecture (HPCA). IEEE; 2015

[13] Nibhanupudi SST, Sundara Raman SR, Cassé M, Hutin L, Kulkarni JP. Ultra-low-voltage UTBB-SOI-based, pseudo-static storage circuits for cryogenic CMOS applications, in IEEE Journal on Exploratory Solid-State Computational Devices and Circuits. Dec. 2021;**7**(2): 201-208. DOI: 10.1109/JXCDC.2021.3130839

[14] Ishiuchi H et al. Embedded DRAM technologies. In: International Electron

Devices Meeting. IEDM Technical Digest. IEEE; 1997

[15] Belmonte A et al. Capacitor-less, long-retention (¿ 400s) DRAM cell paving the way towards low-power and high-density monolithic 3D DRAM. In: 2020 IEEE International Electron Devices Meeting (IEDM). IEEE; 2020

[16] Koob JC et al. Design and characterization of a multilevel DRAM. IEEE Transactions on Very Large Scale Integration (VLSI) Systems. 2010;**19**(9): 1583-1596

[17] Ali MF, Jaiswal A, Roy K. In-memory low-cost bit-serial addition using commodity DRAM technology. IEEE Transactions on Circuits and Systems I: Regular Papers. 2019;**67**(1):155-165

[18] Raman SRS, Xie S, Kulkarni JP. Compute-in-eDRAM with backend integrated indium gallium zinc oxide transistors. In: 2021 IEEE International Symposium on Circuits and Systems (ISCAS). Daegu, Korea: IEEE; 2021. pp. 1-5. DOI: 10.1109/ISCAS51556.2021.9401798

[19] Sundara Raman SR, Xie S, Kulkarni JP. IGZO CIM: Enabling In-memory computations using multilevel Capacitorless indium–gallium–zinc–oxide-based embedded DRAM technology, in IEEE Journal on Exploratory Solid-State Computational Devices and Circuits. June 2022;**8**(1): 35-43. DOI: 10.1109/JXCDC.2022.3188366

[20] Compagnoni CM et al. Reviewing the evolution of the NAND flash technology. Proceedings of the IEEE. 2017;**105**(9):1609-1633

[21] Boppidi PKR, Raman SS, et al. Pt/Cu: ZnO/Nb: STO memristive dual port for cache memory applications. In: AIP Conference Proceedings. Vol. 2265. No. 1. AIP Publishing LLC; 2020

[22] Micheloni R, Crippa L, Marelli A. Inside NAND Flash Memories. Springer Science Business Media; 2010

[23] Li Y, Quader KN. NAND flash memory: Challenges and opportunities. Computer. 2013;**46**(8):23-29

[24] Goda A. Recent progress on 3D NAND flash technologies. Electronics. 2021;**10**(24):3156

[25] Bez R et al. Introduction to flash memory. Proceedings of the IEEE. 2003; **91**(4):489-502

[26] Wong H-SP et al. Metal–oxide RRAM. Proceedings of the IEEE. 2012;**100**(6):1951-1970

[27] Shen Z et al. Advances of RRAM devices: Resistive switching mechanisms, materials and bionic synaptic application. Nanomaterials. 2020;**10**(8):1437

[28] Ielmini D. Modeling the universal set/reset characteristics of bipolar RRAM by field-and temperature-driven filament growth. IEEE Transactions on Electron Devices. 2011;**58**(12):4309-4317

[29] Tehrani S et al. Progress and outlook for MRAM technology. IEEE Transactions on Magnetics. 1999;**35**(5): 2814-2819

[30] Huai Y. Spin-transfer torque MRAM (STT-MRAM): Challenges and prospects. AAPPS Bulletin. 2008;**18**(6): 33-40

[31] Fong X et al. KNACK: A hybrid spin-charge mixed-mode simulator for evaluating different genres of spin-transfer torque MRAM bit-cells. In: 2011

International Conference on Simulation of Semiconductor Processes and Devices. IEEE; 2011

[32] Fong X et al. Spin-transfer torque memories: Devices, circuits, and systems. Proceedings of the IEEE. 2016; **104**(7):1449-1488

[33] Dünkel S et al. A FeFET based super-low-power ultra-fast embedded NVM technology for 22nm FDSOI and beyond. In: 2017 IEEE International Electron Devices Meeting (IEDM). IEEE; 2017

[34] Yurchuk E et al. Charge-trapping phenomena in HfO2-based FeFET-type nonvolatile memories. IEEE Transactions on Electron Devices. 2016; **63**(9):3501-3507

[35] Raman SRS, Nibhanupudi SST, Saha AK, Gupta S, Kulkarni JP. Threshold selector and capacitive coupled assist techniques for write voltage reduction in metal–ferroelectric–metal field-effect transistor. IEEE Transactions on Electron Devices. 2021; **68**(12):6132-6138. DOI: 10.1109/TED.2021.3121348

[36] Lee K, Bae J, Kim S, Lee J, Park B, Kwon D. Ferroelectric gate field-effect transistor memory with Recessed Channel. IEEE Electron Device Letters. 2020;**41**(8):1201-1204

[37] Muller J, Boscke TS, Schroder U, Hoffmann R, Mikolajick T, Frey L. Nanosecond Polarization Switching and Long Retention in a Novel MFIS-FET Based on Ferroelectric HfO_2. IEEE Electron Device Letters. 2012;**33**(2):185-187

Chapter 4

MRAM-Based FPGAs: A Survey

Peyton Chandarana, Mohammed Elbtity, Ronald F. DeMara and Ramtin Zand

Abstract

Over the last decade, field programmable gate arrays (FPGAs) have embraced heterogeneity in a transformative way by leveraging emerging memory devices along with conventional CMOS-based devices to realize technology-specific benefits. Memristive device technologies exhibit desirable characteristics such as non-volatility, scalability, near-zero leakage, radiation hardness, and more, making them promising alternatives for SRAM cells found in conventional SRAM-based FPGAs. In recent years, a significant amount of research has been performed to take advantage of these emerging technologies to develop fundamental building blocks of FPGAs like hybrid CMOS-memristive look-up tables (LUTs) and configurable logic blocks (CLBs). In this chapter, we will provide a brief overview of the previous work on hybrid CMOS-memristive FPGAs and their corresponding opportunities and challenges.

Keywords: magnetoresistive random-access memory (MRAM), non-volatile FPGA, MRAM-based look-up table, hybrid configurable logic block, heterogeneous technology reconfigurable fabric

1. Introduction

Since the advent of the first field programmable gate array (FPGAs), there has been a gradual transition from traditional homogeneous reconfigurable fabrics, designed with one type of logic block, to the now modern heterogeneous FPGAs with special-purpose co-processors to handle specific tasks such as floating point arithmetic [1, 2]. In recent years, a new type of heterogeneity has attracted the attention of both academia and industry which involves leveraging emerging logic and memory devices within FPGA fabrics to realize technology-specific advantages such as non-volatility, scalability, low leakage power, radiation hardness, etc. Some of the most promising technologies that have been proposed as alternatives for static random access memory (SRAM) cells in FPGAs are resistive random-access memory (RRAM) [3–6], phase-change memory (PCM) [7–9], and magnetoresistive random-access memory (MRAM) [10–14]. In this chapter, we specifically focus on MRAM-based FPGAs, but the underlying circuits and architectures discussed can be readily utilized for other resistive memory technologies.

Magnetic tunnel junctions (MTJs) are considered to be the primary component of MRAM devices. **Figure 1** shows an example of the MTJ stack structure [15], which includes two ferromagnetic (FM) layers (CoFeB), called the pinned and free layers,

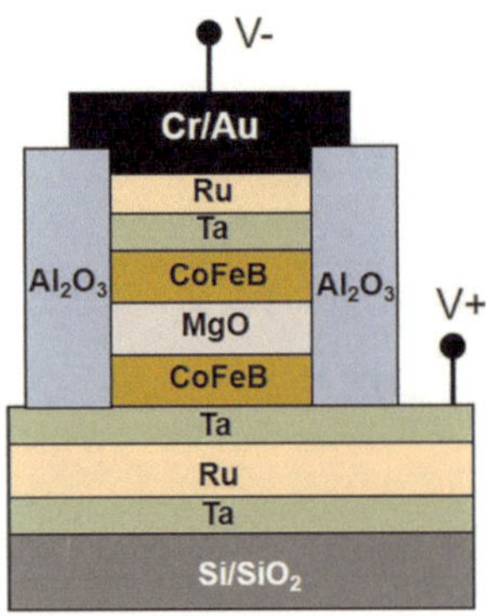

Figure 1.
MTJ stack structure [15].

that are separated by a thin oxide layer (MgO). The magnetization direction of the electrons in the pinned layers is fixed, while that of the free layer can switch to the parallel (P) or anti-parallel (AP) states with reference to the fixed layer. The resistance of an MTJ (R_{MTJ}) depends on the angle between the magnetization orientation of the FM layers (θ), as expressed in the below equation [16]:

$$R_{MTJ}(\theta) = \frac{2R_{Stack}(1 + TMR)}{2 + TMR(1 + \cos\theta)} = \begin{cases} R_P = R_{Stack}, & \theta = 0 \\ R_{AP} = R_{Stack}(1 + TMR), & \theta = \pi \end{cases} \tag{1}$$

where $R_{Stack} = \frac{RA}{Area}$, in which the resistance-area product (RA) value is determined by the material composition of MTJ's layers. Moreover, TMR is the tunneling magnetoresistance, which depends on the temperature (T) and bias voltage (V_b) as seen below [16]:

$$TMR(T, V_b) = \frac{2P^2\left(1 - \alpha_{sp}T^{3/2}\right)^2}{1 - P^2\left(1 - \alpha_{sp}T^{3/2}\right)^2} \cdot \frac{1}{1 + \left(\frac{V_b}{V_0}\right)^2} \tag{2}$$

where V_0 is a fitting parameter, α_{sp} is a material-dependent constant, and P is the spin polarization factor [16]. **Table 1** lists the experimental parameters used herein to model the MTJ devices. Spin transfer torque (STT) [18] is the conventional approach

Parameters	Description	Value
$Area$	MTJ surface	$65nm \times 65nm \times \pi/4$
RA	MTJ resistance-area product	$5\ \Omega.\mu m^2$
T	Temperature	358 K
P	Polarization	0.52
V_0	Fitting parameter	0.65
α_{sp}	Material-dependent constant	2e-5

Table 1.
Parameters of STT-MTJ device [16, 17].

to switch the resistance state of the MTJ, where a bidirectional charge current flows through the fixed layer of the MTJ. This, in turn, generates a spin-polarized current that switches the magnetization orientation of the electrons in the free layer. Recently, it has been shown that passing a charge current through a heavy metal can generate a spin-polarized current with a ratio greater than one [19]. This means the produced spin current can be larger than the applied charge current, and thus, lower energy switching can be achieved in the MRAM cells. Readers can refer to [20] for further details about the fundamentals and modeling of MRAM devices. Proceeding with this background information on MRAM cells, we can now introduce how MRAM technology can be used as an alternative for SRAM to realize the building blocks of FPGAs, such as look-up tables (LUTs) and configurable logic blocks (CLBs).

2. MRAM-based look-up table (LUT) circuits

Look-up tables (LUTs) are the main building blocks in FPGAs that allow combinational and sequential logic circuits to be realized. An n-input LUT circuit includes: (1) 2^n memory cells, containing a truth table of an n-input Boolean logic function, and (2) a select tree used to return the value stored in a specific memory cell specified by an address passed into the LUT circuit. Conventional LUT circuits consist of memory cells implemented using SRAM technology. This, however, introduces multiple challenges with respect to:

- *High static power*: Caused by the intrinsic leakage current which increases as the transistor size decreases.
- *Volatility*: SRAM's volatility limits the energy savings that could be achieved by power-gating in FPGAs. All functions must be reprogrammed upon each power-up, and therefore, external non-volatile memory is needed to reprogram all the functions upon each power-gating cycle.
- *Low logic density*: Each SRAM cell consists of six transistors which increases logic and memory footprint at scale.

In recent years, various MRAM-based LUT circuits have been proposed, where MRAM technology replaces SRAM. Similar to conventional SRAM-based LUTs, MRAM-LUTs have two operation phases: (1) the *configuration phase*, during which the states of the MTJs in MRAM cells are adjusted based on the Boolean logic function being stored in the LUT, and (2) the *read phase*, which involves reading the state of the MTJ devices in the MRAM-LUT to realize a Boolean function. The configuration operation of the MRAM cell requires special write circuitry to generate a sufficiently large spin current to switch the state of the MTJs. **Figure 2** Shows four well-known circuits introduced in the literature for the MRAM write operation.

The LUT read operation, on the other hand, involves sensing the resistive states of MRAM cells and generating the corresponding Boolean outputs, that is, "0" and "1". A commonly used circuit for reading the state of the MTJs is a pre-charge sense amplifier (PCSA) shown in **Figure 3**. The PCSA circuit reads the MTJ states in two steps that could be performed in one clock cycle: (1) the *pre-charge step*, in which the CLK signal is in a low state (GND) that leads to turning the MP0 and MP3 PMOS transistors on, and thus, the OUT and OUT' nodes are charged to VDD, and (2) the *discharge phase*,

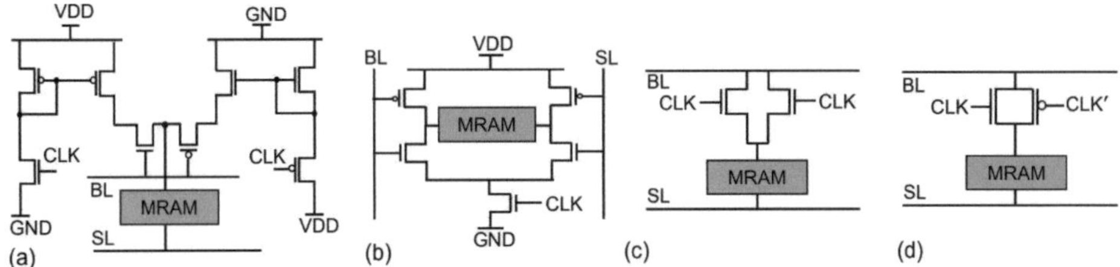

Figure 2.
Various MRAM write circuits circuit structure. (a) Current mirror write circuit [21], (b) proposed in [21], (c) proposed in [22], (d) proposed in [23].

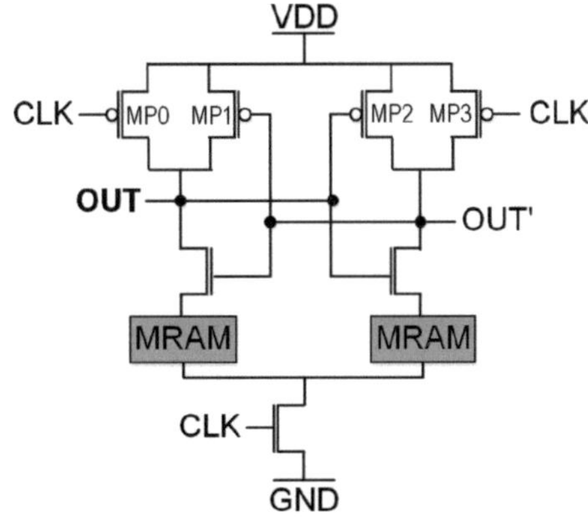

Figure 3.
PCSA circuit schematic.

where CLK signal is in a high state (VDD) which turns off all the PMOS transistors (MP0-MP3) and consequently disconnects the OUT and OUT' nodes from the voltage source (VDD). Therefore, the pre-charged OUT and OUT' nodes begin discharging. The discharge speed in each of the branches of the PCSA relies on the total resistance of each branch which, itself, depends on the resistance of the MRAM device connected to it. The branch of lower resistance discharges faster than the other and therefore turns on the PMOS transistor connected to the branch of higher resistance. This causes the opposite output node of the lower-resistance branch to connect to the VDD, while the output node connected to the lower-resistance branch discharges completely to GND. A comprehensive survey of various PCSA circuits designed for sensing MRAM cells is provided in [24].

One of the pioneering works on MRAM-LUT circuit design belongs to Zhao et al. [25], in which one PCSA circuit is used to sense each bit of the LUT, as shown in **Figure 4a**. The write circuits store each bit of the Boolean function in one MRAM cell and its inverse in another as a reference resistive memory that is used by the PCSA circuit to read the cells. A select tree is then used to read the corresponding MRAM cell, based on the input of the LUT circuit. However, the use of one PCSA per cell in the LUT for reading has led to significant energy and area overheads. Therefore, in 2012, Suzuki et al. [26] proposed an optimized MRAM-LUT design, in which only one PCSA is used in the LUT architecture as shown in **Figure 4b**. One branch of the PCSA is connected to the select tree and LUT MRAM cells, while the other branch is connected to a reference tree and a combination of MRAM devices. Reference tree

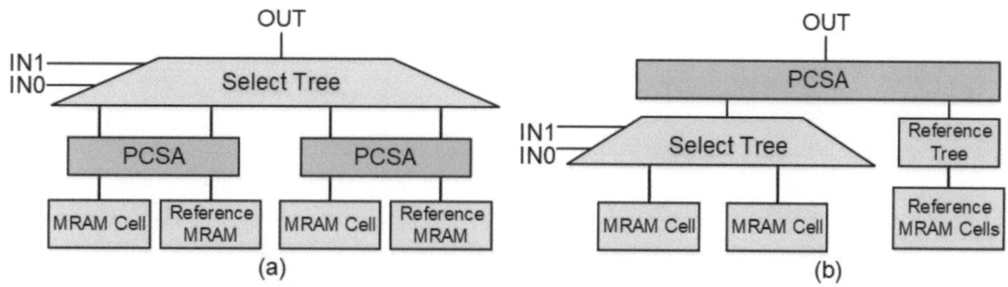

Figure 4.
Basic MRAM-LUT circuit structure: (a) proposed in [25], and (b) proposed in [26].

compensates for the resistance of the select tree and the reference MRAM cells provide a total resistance value between the high resistance (R_{AP}) and low resistance (R_P) of the LUT MRAM cells. With this modification in the circuit, Suzuki et al. [26] achieved a 44% reduction in active power compared to the MRAM-LUT designed in [25]. Another well-known MRAM-LUT circuit is proposed by Zand et al. in [27]. Instead of using multiple MRAM cells to form a reference MRAM cell, Zand et al. adjusted the area of a single MTJ such that its resistance in the parallel (P) state is between the high resistance (R_{AP}) and low resistance (R_P) of the main MRAM cells in the LUT circuit. This simple modification led to a 34% improvement in the power-delay-product (PDP) value compared to the MRAM-LUT design proposed by Suzuki et al. in [26].

2.1 Modern MRAM-LUT circuits

Most modern FPGAs utilize more versatile LUT structures in their architecture compared to the basic designs introduced in the previous subsection. Intel FPGAs, for example, the Arria®series, Cyclone®V, and Stratix®V, use adaptive logic modules (ALMs) as their building blocks. This can simultaneously realize various types of functions such as two independent 4-input functions, a 5-input and a 3-input function, two 5-input functions, which share two inputs, and so on [28]. Similarly, Xilinx FPGAs, for example, the Virtex-7 Family, employ fracturable 6-input LUTs in their design that can realize an independent 6-input function or two 5-input functions, if they share five inputs. Recently, there have been some efforts to design novel MRAM-LUT circuits that can support functionalities similar to those of modern LUT circuits. Here, we focus on two of the well-known designs in this area, that is, *adaptive MRAM-LUT* and *fracturable MRAM-LUT* proposed in [27, 29], respectively.

2.1.1 Adaptive MRAM-LUT design

Figure 5 shows a 4-input adaptive MRAM-LUT circuit proposed in [27], which can be configured to realize different functions. There are seven types of functions that can be implemented by the 4-input adaptive MRAM-LUT: four 2-input Boolean functions, two 3-input functions, and one 4-input function. The output of each configuration is individually connected to the PCSA circuit through a mode selector that includes pass transistors to choose between the different operational modes listed in **Table 2**. For example, in Mode 0, the adaptive MRAM-LUT is configured to operate as a 2-input LUT and realize the logic function stored in MRAM0 thru MRAM3.

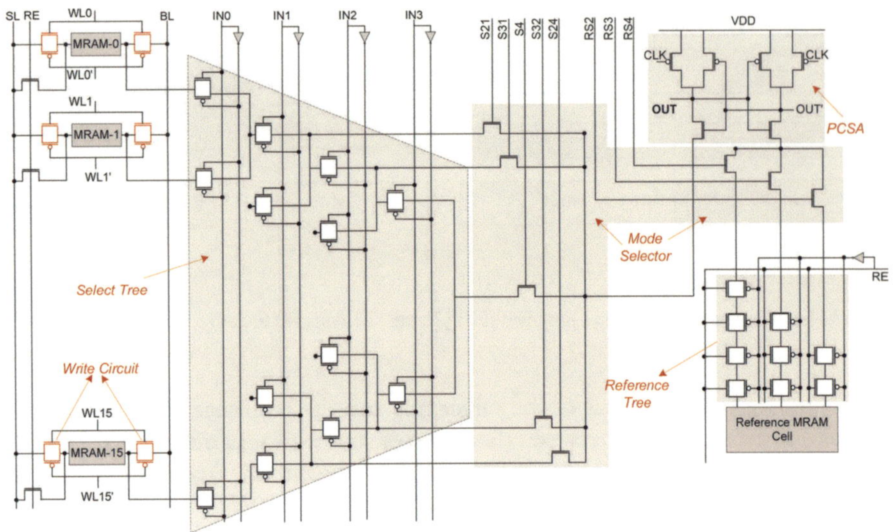

Figure 5.
The circuit diagram of a 4-input adaptive MRAM-LUT [27].

Mode	S21	S22	S23	S24	S31	S32	S4	RS2	RS3	RS4	MRAMs	Function
	1	0	0	0	0	0	0	1	0	0	0–3	2-input
	0	1	0	0	0	0	0	1	0	0	4–7	2-input
	0	0	1	0	0	0	0	1	0	0	8–11	2-input
	0	0	0	1	0	0	0	1	0	0	12–15	2-input
	0	0	0	0	1	0	0	0	1	0	0–7	3-input
	0	0	0	0	0	1	0	0	1	0	8–15	3-input
	0	0	0	0	0	0	1	0	0	1	0–15	4-input

Table 2.
Different operating modes in the 4-input adaptive MRAM-LUT.

2.1.2 Fracturable MRAM-LUT design

Figure 6 shows the structure of a six-input MRAM-LUT circuit proposed in [29], which includes MRAM-based storage cells, a select tree, a mode selector, and two PCSAs. The fracturable MRAM-LUT circuit is capable of implementing any six-input Boolean functions or two five-input Boolean functions if the inputs are shared. The M5 and M6 signals are used to select the 5-input or 6-input functional modes of the fracturable MRAM-LUT circuit, respectively. Zand and DeMara [30] have shown that fracturable MRAM-LUT circuits can achieve significant reductions in power consumption compared to their SRAM-based counterparts. However, they have also shown that MRAM-LUTs can be severely impacted by process variation (PV), while SRAM-LUTs exhibit no read errors in presence of PV.

There have been several efforts to address the PV challenges of MRAM-LUTs including the proposal of modular redundancy-based MRAM-LUT and clock-less MRAM-LUT circuits proposed in [30, 31], respectively. In [30], the authors identified the PCSA circuit as the most susceptible component of the MRAM-LUT and as a

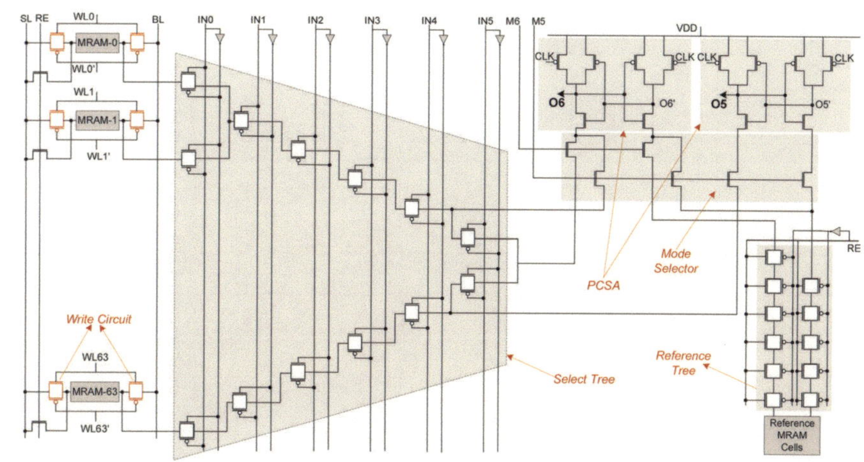

Figure 6.
The circuit diagram of a six-input fracturable MRAM-LUT [30].

result, proposed a triple modular redundancy method to alleviate the PV impacts. As shown in **Figure 7**, the proposed circuit includes three PCSAs and two voter circuits that determine the output of the LUT circuit based on the majority of the PCSA's outputs. The modular redundancy-based MRAM-LUT could successfully decrease the PV-induced read errors by more than 30% at the cost of a 24% and 6% increase in power consumption and area occupation, respectively.

In another effort to reduce the impact of PV on MRAM-LUT circuits, Salehi et al. [31] propose a fracturable MRAM-LUT design that uses two MRAM cells with differential magnetization polarities to represent each bit of the Boolean function stored in the LUT. This enables replacing the PCSA circuits, which are the main source of errors caused by PV in MRAM-LUTs, with a voltage divider circuit to read the states of the MTJs, as shown in **Figure 8**. Since the values stored in the MRAM cells are complementary, that is, one MRAM device is used to store the data value and the other as a reference, a wide read margin is realized, and this leads to a near zero error rate for the MRAM-LUT circuit in presence of various PV scenarios in both transistor and MRAM devices. However, as shown by Salehi et al. [31], PV-tolerance is achieved at the cost of increased power consumption compared to the PCSA-based MRAM-LUTs.

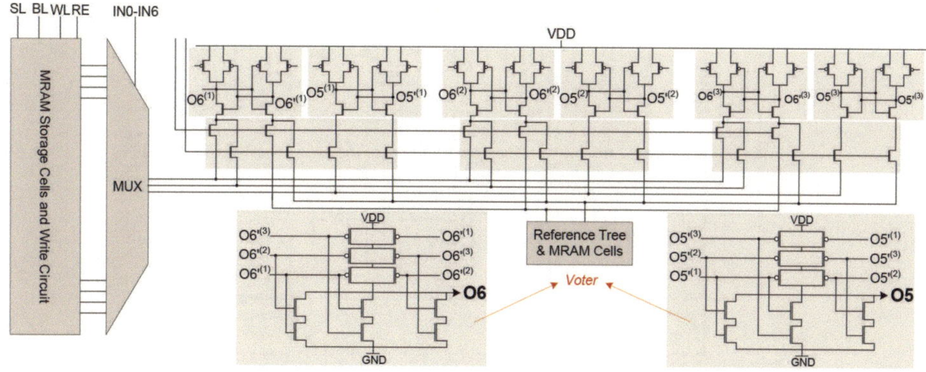

Figure 7.
The circuit diagram of a six-input modular redundancy-based fracturable MRAM-LUT [30].

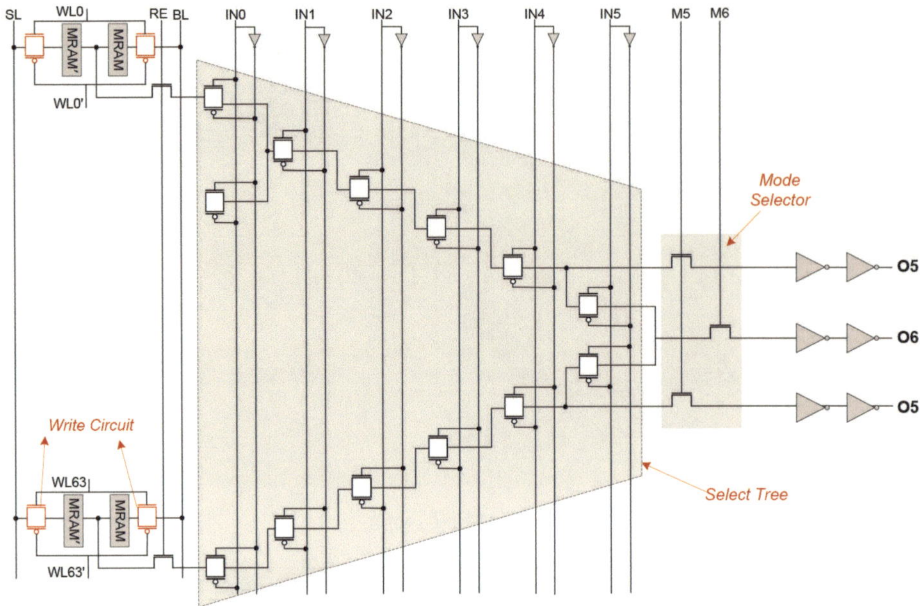

Figure 8.
The circuit diagram of a six-input fracturable MRAM-LUT that uses voltage divider circuits instead of PCSAs for the LUT's read operation [31].

3. MRAM-based FPGAs

Figure 9 shows the typical architecture of modern FPGAs, which include configurable logic blocks (CLBs), input–output blocks (IOBs), block RAMs, programmable switch matrices (SMs), and delay-locked loops (DLLs) for clock distribution. Bitstreams are used to store the logic functions in CLBs. Any new design of FPGAs that

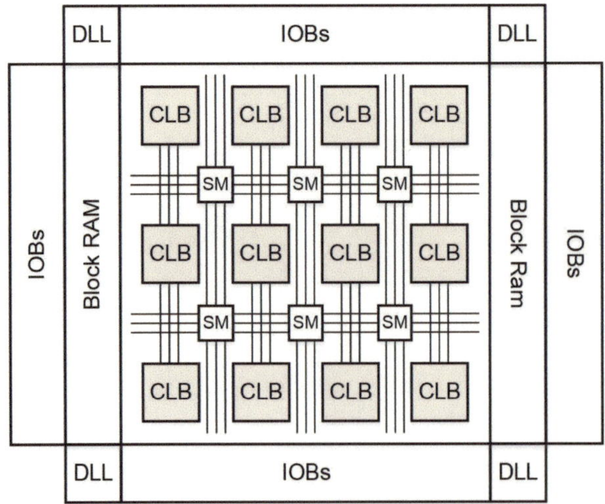

Figure 9.
A typical FPGA architecture.

intend to use MRAM-LUT circuits in their structure is desired to have the highest compatibility with modern FPGAs such that similar routing structures, programming paradigms, and toolchains can still be leveraged with minimal modifications. In [12], Zand and DeMara propose a hybrid spin/charge-based FPGA (HSC-FPGA) which is based on the architecture of Xilinx FPGAs, such as the Virtex 7 family.

Similar to the CLBs in modern Xilinx FPGAs, the CLBs in HSC-FPGA provide logic circuits including (1) six-input LUT circuit, (2) dual five-input LUTs with shared inputs, (3) distributed memory, (4) shift registers, and (5) dedicated carry logic for arithmetic operations. In particular, as shown in **Figure 10**, the HSC-FPGA's CLB architecture includes two slices to implement sequential and combinational logic functions, called Slice-S and Slice-C, respectively. Slice-C consists of SRAM-based LUT circuits that can also be used as shift registers and distributed RAM. Slice-S includes six-input fracturable MRAM-LUTs as well as latch and flip-flop circuits to realize sequential logic. Suzuki and Hanyu [32] have designed an MRAM-LUT circuit that can also operate as a shift register, however, they consume significantly higher energy compared to SRAM-based shift registers due to the high switching energy required to change the state of the MRAM cells. Overall, the simulation results, in [12], show that the HSC-FPGA can achieve more than 18% reduction in area occupation, in addition to a 70% and 15% decrease in standby power and read power dissipation, respectively, compared to conventional SRAM-based FPGAs.

Besides the designs discussed in this chapter, there are several important efforts in this area at different levels of design abstraction, from circuit and architecture to the fabrication of FPGA chips, with different design objectives including but not limited to: increasing performance, reducing power, area, and improving reliability and security. **Table 3** lists some of these efforts in the past two decades which have advanced the area of research, achieved promising results and set the foundation for future research and manufacturing of MRAM-based FPGAs.

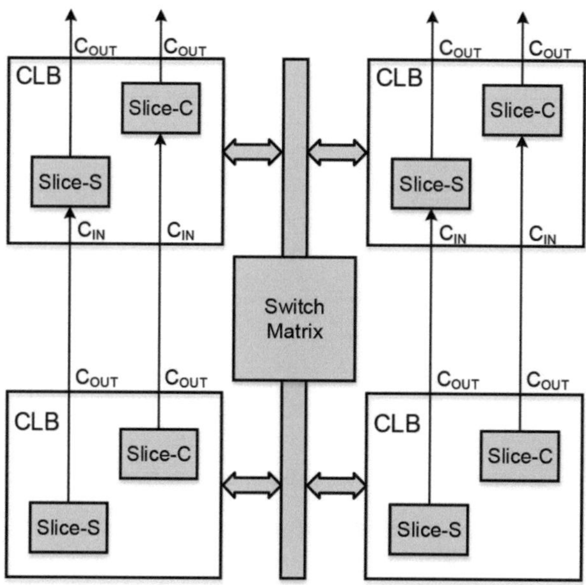

Figure 10.
The structure of the CLBs in hybrid spin-charge FPGA proposed in [12].

Paper	Design level			Design objective				
	Cir	Arch	Fab	Speed	Area	Power	Reliability	Security
[33]	✓					✓	✓	
[34]	✓	✓		✓	✓			
[35]	✓	✓	✓		✓	✓	✓	
[36]	✓		✓	✓		✓		
[37]	✓			✓	✓	✓		✓
[29]	✓			✓		✓	✓	
[38]	✓					✓		
[39]	✓		✓	✓				
[27]	✓			✓		✓		
[40]	✓		✓	✓	✓	✓		
[41]	✓			✓		✓	✓	
[26]	✓				✓			
[42]	✓	✓	✓			✓		
[10]	✓		✓		✓	✓		
[43]	✓		✓	✓		✓		
[44]	✓	✓	✓	✓		✓		
[30]	✓	✓			✓	✓	✓	
[45]		✓		✓		✓		
[46]	✓			✓		✓		
[47]	✓	✓		✓	✓	✓	✓	
[48]		✓			✓	✓	✓	
[49]				✓	✓	✓	✓	
[50]		✓		✓		✓		
[51]	✓		✓		✓	✓		✓
[52]	✓			✓		✓		
[13]	✓			✓		✓	✓	
[53]		✓			✓	✓	✓	✓
[11]	✓		✓	✓	✓	✓	✓	

Table 3.
An overview of the MRAM-based FPGA designs in the past two decades.

4. Conclusions

In this chapter, we provided an overview of the recent efforts in developing the next generation of FPGA fabrics which take advantage of the cooperating strengths of CMOS technology, such as fast and energy-efficient switching, and MRAM technology to attain characteristics such as non-volatility and low standby power. The prior research in this area shows that MRAM-based FPGAs can achieve significant reductions in power consumption and chip area compared to conventional SRAM-based FPGAs. However, further research is required for addressing the reliability challenges of MRAM-based FPGAs including susceptibility to process variation, and endurance of memristive devices which can impact the reprogrammability of the FPGAs. Finally, this area of research provides several possibilities for future work, such as developing memristive-based in-memory computing co-processors to handle data-intensive applications such as machine learning and graph processing in hybrid memristive-CMOS FPGAs.

Abbreviations

FPGA	Field programmable gate array
CMOS	Complementary metal-oxide-semiconductor
SRAM	Static random-access memory
LUT	Look-up table
CLB	Configurable logic blocks
RRAM	Resistive random-access memory
PCM	Phase-change memory
MRAM	Magnetoresistive random-access memory
MTJ	Magnetic tunnel junctions
FM	Ferro-magnetic
CoFeB	Cobalt-ferrous-foron
MgO	Magnesium-oxide
P	Parallel
AP	Anti-parallel
RA	Resistance-area product
TMR	Tunneling magnetoresistance
STT	Spin transfer torque
PCSA	Pre-charge sense amplifier
PMOS	P-channel metal–oxide-semiconductor
PDP	Power-delay-product
ALM	Adaptive logic modules
PV	Process variation
IOB	Input–output block
SM	Switch matrix
DLL	Delay-locked loop
HSC	Hybrid spin/charge
EDA	Electronic design automation

Author details

Peyton Chandarana[1†], Mohammed Elbtity[1†], Ronald F. DeMara[2] and Ramtin Zand[1*]

1 University of South Carolina, Columbia, United States

2 University of Central Florida, Orlando, United States

*Address all correspondence to: ramtin@cse.sc.edu

† These authors contributed equally.

References

[1] DeMara RF, Roohi A, Zand R, Pyle SD. Heterogeneous technology configurable fabrics for field-programmable co-design of cmos and spin-based devices. In: 2017 IEEE International Conference on Rebooting Computing (ICRC). Washington, DC, USA: IEEE; 2017. pp. 1-4

[2] Kuon I, Tessier R, Rose J, et al. Fpga architecture: Survey and challenges. Foundations and Trends® in Electronic Design Automation. 2008;**2**(2):135-253

[3] Cong J, Xiao B. Fpga-rpi: A novel fpga architecture with rram-based programmable interconnects. IEEE Transactions on Very Large Scale Integration (VLSI) Systems. 2013;**22**(4): 864-877

[4] Liauw YY, Zhang Z, Kim W, El Gamal A, Wong SS. Nonvolatile 3d-fpga with monolithically stacked rram-based configuration memory. In: 2012 IEEE International Solid-State Circuits Conference. San Francisco, California, USA: IEEE; 2012. pp. 406-408

[5] Tanachutiwat S, Liu M, Wang W. Fpga based on integration of cmos and rram. IEEE Transactions on Very Large Scale Integration (VLSI) Systems. 2010; **19**(11):2023-2032

[6] Chen Y-C, Wang W, Li H, Zhang W. Non-volatile 3d stacking rram-based fpga. In: 22nd International Conference on Field Programmable Logic and Applications (FPL). Oslo, Norway: IEEE; 2012. pp. 367-372

[7] Huang K, Ha Y, Zhao R, Kumar A, Lian Y. A low active leakage and high reliability phase change memory (pcm) based non-volatile fpga storage element. IEEE Transactions on Circuits and Systems I: Regular Papers. 2014;**61**(9):2605-2613

[8] Chen Y, Zhao J, Xie Y. 3d-nonfar: Three-dimensional non-volatile fpga architecture using phase change memory. In: Proceedings of the 16th ACM/IEEE International Symposium on Low Power Electronics and Design. Austin, Texas, USA: Association for Computing Machinery (ACM); 2010. pp. 55-60

[9] Gaillardon P-E, Ben-Jamaa MH, Beneventi GB, Clermidy F, Perniola L. Emerging memory technologies for reconfigurable routing in fpga architecture. In: 2010 17th IEEE International Conference on Electronics, Circuits and Systems. IEEE; 2010. pp. 62-65

[10] Suzuki D, Natsui M, Mochizuki A, Miura S, Honjo H, Sato H, et al. Fabrication of a 3000-6-input-luts embedded and block-level power-gated nonvolatile fpga chip using p-mtj-based logic-in-memory structure. In: 2015 Symposium on VLSI Circuits (VLSI Circuits). Kyoto, Japan: IEEE; 2015. pp. C172-C173

[11] Zhao W, Belhaire E, Chappert C, Mazoyer P. Spin transfer torque (stt)-mram–based runtime reconfiguration fpga circuit. ACM Transactions on Embedded Computing Systems. 2009;**9**: 14:1-14:16

[12] Zand R, DeMara RF. Hsc-fpga: A hybrid spin/charge fpga leveraging the cooperating strengths of cmos and mtj devices. In: Proceedings of the 2019 ACM/SIGDA International Symposium on Field-Programmable Gate Arrays, Ser. FPGA'19. New York, NY, USA: Association for Computing Machinery; 2019. pp. 118-119. DOI: 10.1145/ 3289602.3293940

[13] Zand R, DeMara RF. Radiation-hardened mram-based lut for

non-volatile fpga soft error mitigation with multi-node upset tolerance. Journal of Physics D: Applied Physics. 2017; **50**(50):505002

[14] Krishna MKG, Roohi A, Zand R, DeMara RF. Heterogeneous energy-sparing reconfigurable logic: Spin-based storage and cnfet-based multiplexing. IET Circuits, Devices & Systems. 2017; **11**(3):274-279

[15] Ikeda S, Miura K, Yamamoto H, Mizunuma K, Gan H, Endo M, et al. A perpendicular-anisotropy cofeb–mgo magnetic tunnel junction. Nature Materials. 2010;**9**(9):721

[16] Zhang Y, Zhao W, Lakys Y, Klein JO, Kim JV, Ravelosona D, et al. Compact modeling of perpendicular-anisotropy cofeb/mgo magnetic tunnel junctions. IEEE Transactions on Electron Devices. 2012;**59**(3):819-826

[17] Kim J, Chen A, Behin-Aein B, Kumar S, Wang J, Kim CH. A technology-agnostic mtj spice model with user-defined dimensions for stt-mram scalability studies. In: 2015 IEEE Custom Integrated Circuits Conference (CICC). San Jose, CA, United States: IEEE; 2015. pp. 1-4

[18] Slonczewski J. Current-driven excitation of magnetic multilayers. Journal of Magnetism and Magnetic Materials. 1996;**159**(1):L1-L7

[19] Liu L, Pai C, Li Y, Tseng HW, Ralph DC, Buhrman RA. Spin-torque switching with the giant spin hall effect of tantalum. Science. 2012;**336**(6081): 555-558

[20] Zand R, Roohi A, DeMara RF. Fundamentals, modeling, and application of magnetic tunnel junctions. In: Nanoscale Devices. Boca Raton, Florida: CRC Press; 2018. pp. 337-368

[21] Ben-Romdhane N, Zhao W, Zhang Y, Klein J-O, Wang Z, Ravelosona D. Design and analysis of racetrack memory based on magnetic domain wall motion in nanowires. In: 2014 IEEE/ACM International Symposium on Nanoscale Architectures (NANOARCH). Paris, France: IEEE; 2014. pp. 71-76

[22] Gupta SK, Park SP, Mojumder NN, Roy K. Layout-aware optimization of stt mrams. In: 2012 Design, Automation & Test in Europe Conference & Exhibition (DATE). Dresden, Germany: IEEE; 2012. pp. 1455-1458

[23] Zand R, Roohi A, DeMara RF. Energy-efficient and process-variation-resilient write circuit schemes for spin hall effect mram device. IEEE Transactions on Very Large Scale Integration (VLSI) Systems. 2017;**25**(9): 2394-2401

[24] Salehi S, Fan D, Demara RF. Survey of stt-mram cell design strategies: Taxonomy and sense amplifier tradeoffs for resiliency. ACM Journal on Emerging Technologies in Computing Systems (JETC). 2017;**13**(3):1-16

[25] Zhao W, Belhaire E, Chappert C, Jacquet F, Mazoyer P. New non-volatile logic based on spin-mtj. physica status solidi (a). 2008;**205**(6):1373-1377

[26] Suzuki D, Natsui M, Hanyu T. Area-efficient lut circuit design based on asymmetry of mtj's current switching for a nonvolatile fpga. In: 2012 IEEE 55th International Midwest Symposium on Circuits and Systems (MWSCAS). Boise, Idaho, USA: IEEE; 2012. pp. 334-337

[27] Zand R, Roohi A, Salehi S, DeMara RF. Scalable adaptive spintronic reconfigurable logic using area-matched mtj design. IEEE Transactions on

Circuits and Systems II: Express Briefs. 2016;**63**(7):678-682

[28] Intel. Adaptive logic module (alm) definition. [Online]. Available from: https://www.intel.com/content/www/us/en/programmable/quartushelp/17.0/reference/glossary/def_alm.htm

[29] Zand R, Roohi A, Fan D, DeMara RF. Energy-efficient nonvolatile reconfigurable logic using spin hall effect-based lookup tables. IEEE Transactions on Nanotechnology. 2017; **16**(1):32-43

[30] Zand R, Demara RF. Mram-enhanced low power reconfigurable fabric with multi-level variation tolerance. IEEE Transactions on Circuits and Systems I: Regular Papers. 2019;**66**: 4662-4672

[31] Salehi S, Zand R, DeMara RF. Clockless spin-based look-up tables with wide read margin. In: Proceedings of the 2019 on Great Lakes Symposium on VLSI. Washington, DC: ACM; 2019. pp. 363-366

[32] Suzuki D, Hanyu T. Design of a magnetic-tunnel-junction-oriented nonvolatile lookup table circuit with write-operation-minimized data shifting. Japanese Journal of Applied Physics. 2018;**57**(4S):04FE09

[33] Lakys Y, Zhao W, Klein J-O, Chappert C. Hardening techniques for mram-based nonvolatile latches and logic. IEEE Transactions on Nuclear Science. 2012;**59**:1136-1141

[34] Zhao W, Belhaire E, Javerliac V, Chappert C, Diény B. Evaluation Ofanon-volatile Fpgabased on Mram Technology. Padua, Italy: IEEE; 2006

[35] Goncalves O, Prenat G, di Pendina G, Diény B. Non-volatile fpgas based on spintronic devices. In: 2013 50th ACM/EDAC/IEEE Design Automation Conference (DAC). Austin, TX, USA: IEEE; 2013. pp. 1-3

[36] Guillemenet Y, Torres L, Sassatelli G, Bruchon N, Hassoune I. A non-volatile run-time fpga using thermally assisted switching mrams. In: 2008 International Conference on Field Programmable Logic and Applications. Heidelberg, Germany: IEEE; 2008. pp. 421-426

[37] Zhao WS, Belhaire E, Mistral Q, Nicolle E, Devolder T, Chappert C. Integration of spin-ram technology in fpga circuits. In: 2006 8th International Conference on Solid-State and Integrated Circuit Technology Proceedings. Shanghai, China: IEEE; 2006. pp. 799-802

[38] Faber L-B, Zhao W, Klein J-O, Devolder T, Chappert C. Dynamic compact model of spin-transfer torque based magnetic tunnel junction (mtj). In: 2009 4th International Conference on Design & Technology of Integrated Systems in Nanoscal era. Cairo, Egypt: IEEE; 2009. pp. 130-135

[39] Silva V, Fernandes JR, Oliveira LB, Neto HC, Ferreira R, Freitas S, et al. Thermal assisted switching magnetic tunnel junctions as fpga memory elements. In: 2009 MIXDES-16th International Conference Mixed Design of Integrated Circuits & Systems. Lodz, Poland: IEEE; 2009. pp. 332-336

[40] Zhao W, Belhaire E, Chappert C, Mazoyer P. Power and area optimization for run-time reconfiguration system on programmable chip based on magnetic random access memory. IEEE Transactions on Magnetics. 2009;**45**:776-780

[41] Rajaei R, Gholipour A. Low power, reliable, and nonvolatile msram cell for

facilitating power gating and nonvolatile dynamically reconfiguration. IEEE Transactions on Nanotechnology. 2018; **17**:261-267

[42] Guillemenet Y, Torres L, Sassatelli G. Non-volatile run-time field-programmable gate arrays structures using thermally assisted switching magnetic random access memories. IET Computers and Digital Techniques. 2010;**4**:211-226

[43] Guillemenet Y, Torres L, Sassatelli G, Bruchon N. On the use of magnetic rams in field-programmable gate arrays. Int. J. Reconfigurable Comput. 2008;**2008**:723 950:1-723 950:9

[44] Bruchon N, Torres L, Sassatelli G, Cambon G. Magnetic tunnelling junction based fpga. In: FPGA'06. Monterey, California, USA: ACM; 2006

[45] Chaudhuri S, Zhao W, Klein J-O, Chappert C, Mazoyer P. High density asynchronous lut based on non-volatile mram technology. In: 2010 International Conference on Field Programmable Logic and Applications. Milan, Italy: IEEE; 2010. pp. 374-379

[46] Hāmsa S, Thangadurai N, Ananth A. Composition of magnetic tunnel junction-based magnetoresistive random access memory for field-programmable gate array. Current Science. Bangalore, India. 2020

[47] Cho K, Lee S, Lee CK, Yim T, Yoon H. Low power multi-context look-up table (lut) using spin-torque transfer magnetic ram for non-volatile fpga. In: 2017 International SoC Design Conference (ISOCC). Seoul, Korea (South): IEEE; 2017. pp. 107-108

[48] Goncalves O, Prenat G, Diény B. Radiation hardened mram-based fpga. IEEE Transactions on Magnetics. 2013; **49**:4355-4358

[49] Rajaei R. Radiation-hardened design of nonvolatile mram-based fpga. IEEE Transactions on Magnetics. 2016;**52**:1-10

[50] Kim J, Song Y, Cho K, Lee H, Yoon H, Chung E-Y. Stt-mram-based multicontext fpga for multithreading computing environment. IEEE Transactions on Computer-Aided Design of Integrated Circuits and Systems. 2022; **41**:1330-1343

[51] Zhao W, Belhaire E, Chappert C, Diény B, Prenat G. Tas-mram-based low-power high-speed runtime reconfiguration (rtr) fpga. ACM Trans. Reconfigurable Technol. Syst. 2009;**2**:8: 1-8:19

[52] Bagheriye L, Toofan S, Saeidi R, Zeinali B, Moradi F. A reduced store/restore energy mram-based sram cell for a non-volatile dynamically reconfigurable fpga. IEEE Transactions on Circuits and Systems II: Express Briefs. 2018;**65**:1708-1712

[53] Goncalves O, Prenat G, Pendina GD, Layer C, Diény B. Nonvolatile runtime-reconfigurable fpga secured through mram-based periodic refresh. In: 2013 5th IEEE International Memory Workshop. Monterey, CA, USA: IEEE; 2013. pp. 170-173

Chapter 5

New Content Addressable Memory Architecture for Multi-Core Applications

Allam Abumwais and Mahmoud Obaid

Abstract

The future of massively parallel computation appears promising due to the emergence of multi- and many-core computers. However, major progress is still needed in terms of the shared memory multi- and many-core systems, specifically in the shared cache memory architecture and interconnection network. When multiple cores try to access the same shared module in the shared cache memory, issues arise. Cache replacement methods and developments in cache architecture have been explored as solutions to this. This chapter introduces the Near-Far Access Replacement Algorithm (NFRA), a new hardware-based replacement technique, as well as a novel dedicated pipeline cache memory design for multi-core processors, known as dual-port content addressable memory (DPCAM). The experiments show that the access latency for write/read operations of a DPCAM is lower than that of a set-associative (SA) cache memory, with the latency of a write operation staying the same regardless of the size of the DPCAM. It is estimated that the power usage will be 7% greater than a SA cache memory of the same size.

Keywords: multi-core processor, shared cache, cache architecture, dual port CAM, replacement algorithm

1. Introduction

The purpose of the special purpose shared memory architecture discussed in this chapter is to allow multiple cores of a multi-core processor to access a cache memory simultaneously, thus decreasing access latency compared to set-associative (SA) caches. This proposed architecture is based on CAM and a new replacement algorithm. In Section 1, the introduction of shared memory types in computer design is discussed, and Section 2 covers the architectures of the DPCAM and the Near-Far Access NFRA. Section 3 provides functional and timing simulation results, power estimation analysis, and an FPGA implementation of the DPCAM.

Multi-core ICs package multiple processors into a single device. Many-core systems, an evolution of multi-core technology, provide intense parallel processing capabilities for a large number of cores. In order for many-core systems to work, shared memory must be used to communicate between the cores. However, this shared memory can become problematic if multiple cores attempt to access it simultaneously. To address this issue, there have been various studies conducted in the literature that aims to reduce latency and power usage when accessing shared memory. Two potential methods for this are improving cache replacement algorithms and optimizing cache architecture.

Many multi-core systems utilize Associative Memory (AM) cache as a way to share memory [1, 2]. The architecture of enhanced caching seeks to facilitate parallel searching and faster retrieval [3]. In contrast, replacement algorithms are employed to aid the cache controller in deciding which data to eliminate in order to make space for new data [4, 5]. Moreover, an effective replacement algorithm can reduce the latency of cache access. Content addressable memory (CAM) is a type of AM that accesses memory locations by comparing tags (parts of the content) rather than calculating the address and has certain properties that make it suitable for use as a shared memory [3, 6, 7]. The use of CAM memory in shared memory for multi-core systems is interesting, as demonstrated by other relevant articles that have recently been published by the authors [8, 9].

1.1 Types of shared cache memory

In contrast to traditional memory architectures, such as Static Random Access Memory (SRAM) and Dynamic RAM (DRAM), which use unique addresses to retrieve and store data, content-operated memory (COM) uses a different approach. COM allows stored data to be accessed based on part of its content, instead of an address [1]. COM is used in a variety of digital computer applications, from branch prediction techniques to very-high-speed parallel systems, to perform two primary memory-related operations: writing (storing data) and reading (accessing the correct corresponding data) when the address is not known [3]. The major application of COMs is packet switching routing and classification on network systems [10]. It is anticipated that COM memory will be used in upcoming applications for non-CMOS next-generation electronic devices [3]. COM memory architectures can be divided into two main categories: AM and CAM. Both of these types of memory perform the same functions, but they do so in different ways.

AM memory is further divided into three categories: direct-mapped (DM), set associative (SA), and fully associative (FA). Each of these memory types has different restrictions on where data can be written, as well as different replacement algorithms that are used. DM memory only allows for one location for a particular data item. FA memory allows for data to be mapped to any location. SA memory allows for a set of possible locations for data to be stored. In the following subsections, a brief overview of each of these three main types of cache memory will be provided.

1.1.1 Fully associative memory

The FA cache memory design stores the address and data in the same cache location, and compares the incoming address with all addresses stored within each location. As shown in **Figure 1**, this type of caching architecture is associated with high performance in comparison with its size; however, its design complexity is a major drawback. To counteract this, Random, First in First out (FIFO), and the Least Recently Used (LRU) algorithms are employed to determine where data should be stored [2].

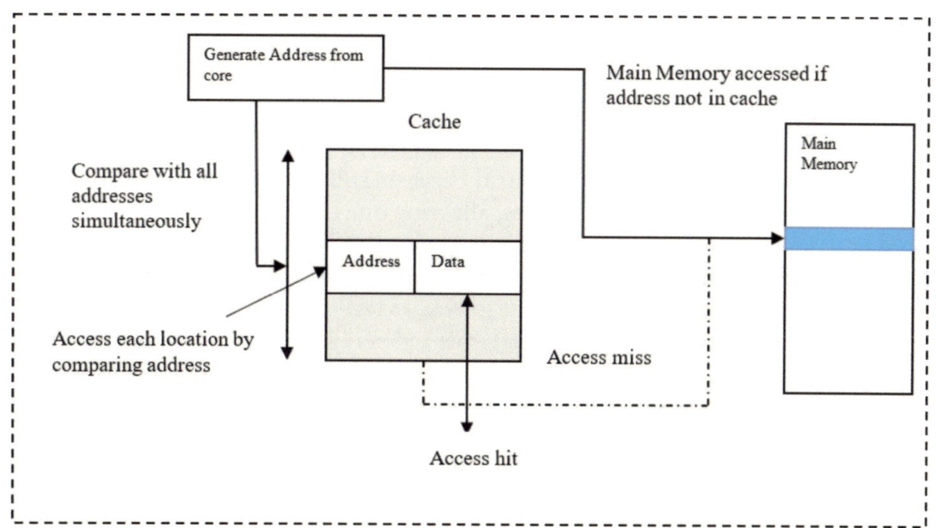

Figure 1.
FA architecture.

FA caches are rarely utilized in multi-core processors due to their lower cache hit rate. Whenever a new memory is referenced to the same cache location, the cache line is replaced, leading to an increased miss rate [1, 2].

1.1.2 Direct mapped memory

In this type of system, the main memory is divided into blocks, and the cache is divided into a set of lines. This means that each cache line can hold one block of the main memory. Rather than storing the full address in the address field, only a part of the address bits is stored alongside the data field [1, 2] shown in **Figure 2**. Direct mapped caching has the benefit of being both simple and cost-effective to implement;

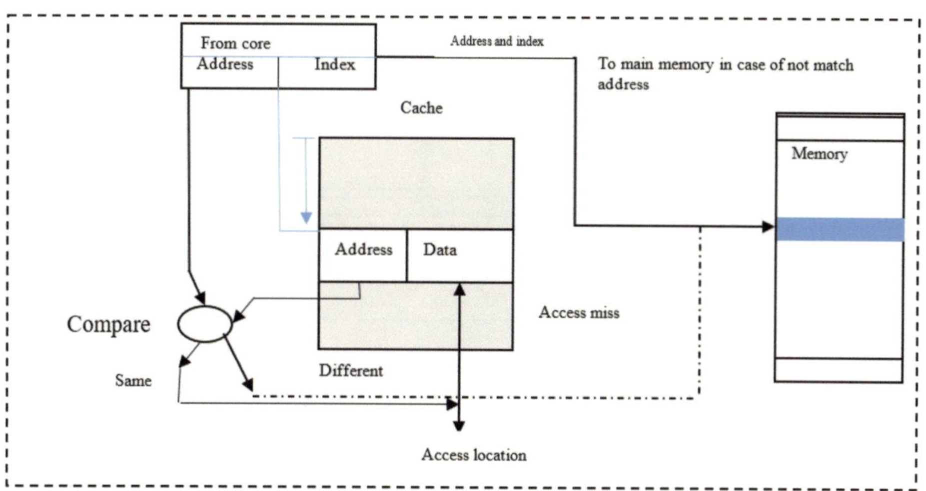

Figure 2.
Direct mapped cache memory.

however, if access to different locations with the same index is attempted, its performance will suffer.

1.1.3 Set-associative memory

Set-associative (SA) caching is a hybrid between full associativity and direct mapping. It splits the cache into a set of lines, allowing one block of main memory to be stored in n potential sets. Compared to a FA cache, it is less complex and can provide better performance since multiple addresses can be stored under the same index. However, its cost increases as the set size grows, as well as its access latency since it has to compare each address in all sets after its index is generated. Despite this, many commercial multi-core systems still use SA caches due to their improved performance [1, 2]. **Figure 3** represents the SA cache memory.

In both FA mapping and SA mapping, there are multiple options for where data can be stored, so replacement algorithms must be used to decide which location should be chosen.

1.1.4 Content-addressable memory

CAM is a type of memory whose locations can be accessed by comparing tags that are parts of the contents, rather than supplying their addresses. In some ways, CAM is similar to direct memory (DM) in its form; both allow for the instant retrieval of an output based on the input. However, both DM and CAM use different methods to facilitate the parallel search and quick storage [2, 3]. DM prevents the storage of particular data in just one location; conversely, CAM has no bounds on where data can be stored. Similarly, CAM and FA are comparable in that they both have no constraint on where data can be saved. Additionally, they both use analogous update and replacement strategies such as random, FIFO, and LRU to replace data when memory is full or the data becomes no longer useful. These algorithms will select a line that is unlikely to be needed in the near future, from all the lines stored in memory [5].

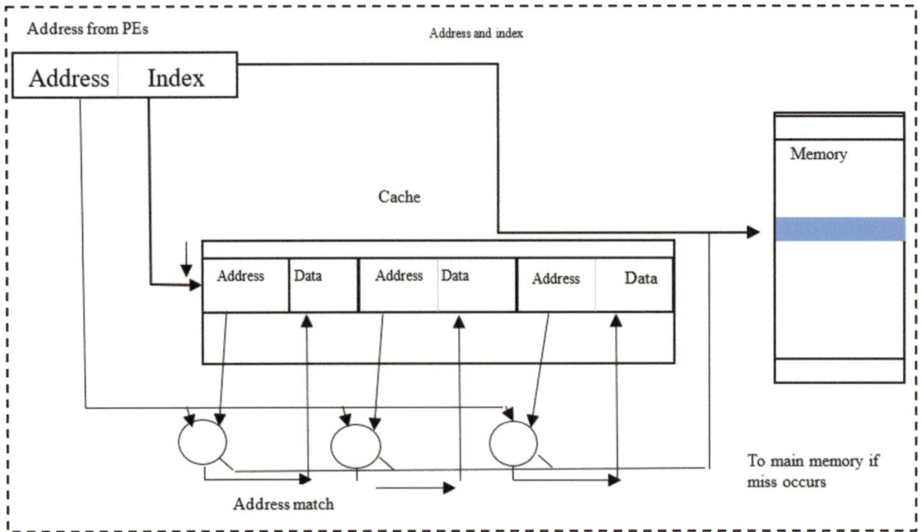

Figure 3.
SA cache memory.

Transactional memory (TM) is a new, emerging type of memory associated with CAM. It is not much different from CAM, but it is used to allow data sharing between processors in a distributed system. TM is used as autonomous storage memory with various hardware components [11, 12].

CAM memory is used for a variety of applications, including image processing, signal processing, pattern recognition, switching network techniques, and parallel processing systems. Unlike traditional SRAM, CAM memory searches through the content of data rather than its address, allowing for parallel and simultaneous search. This makes it a powerful tool that can quickly search through memory contents [3, 13–15].

A unique tag is assigned to each data in a CAM. To read the data, a read signal and the tag are applied to all locations at the same time, and then, the applied tag is compared with all of the previously stored tags. If a match is found, the data in the matched location is selected, output on the data bus, and read by the core. **Figure 4** displays the architecture of a CAM with a single port. It was not previously possible to make CAMs as a standalone memory in any system because a large number of pins were required; however, with the advances in semiconductor technology and FPGAs, researchers are now able to implement CAMs in FPGAs [7, 16]. These types of memory improve the search rate and reduce the processing latency and sometimes the power consumption.

The SA cache is the most popular architecture type used as shared memory in multi-core systems [1, 3]. It still suffers from many problems such as increasing access latency and contention if more than one core tries to access the same shared memory simultaneously. These problems are solved using the proposed DPCAM architecture.

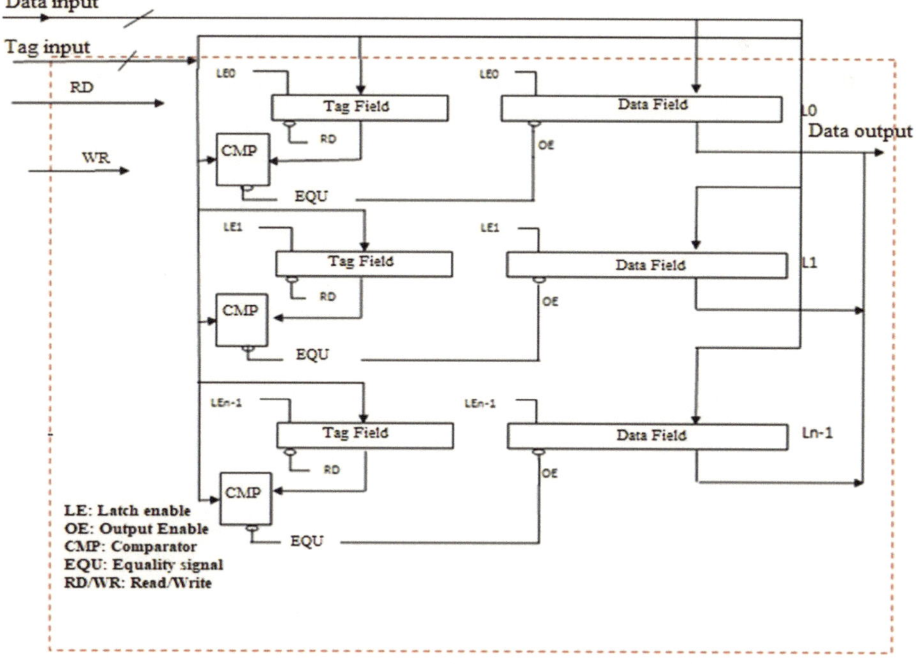

Figure 4.
CAM architecture.

2. Proposed DPCAM

As demonstrated in **Figure 5**, a Dual-Port Content Addressable Memory (DPCAM) can be used with a separate, pipelined shared cache. A Tag Field, Data Field, control unit (CU), comparator (CMP), Tag Field, Data Field, and two ports (Ds_{31}-Ds_0 for writing and Dd_{31}–Dd_0 for reading) are all included in the cache. The core sends Data source [Ds_{31}–Ds_0] and Tag source [Ts_{15}–Ts_0] to be written to the chosen cache line during the Store Back (SB) stage. The cached data is read to the destination data bus [Dd31–Dd0] during the Operand Fetch (OF) step, while the core simultaneously sends the Tag destination [Td_{15}–Td_0] for comparison with each cache line. Both ports have the ability to operate simultaneously.

The Data Field and the Tag Field are the two components that make up a cache line (L). The common data is kept in the Data Field, and each Data Field's specific tag (data and version number) is kept in the Tag Field. Depending on the sort of architecture the CAM is used in, the length of each field can be altered. A 24-bit tag, for instance, can hold up to 16 Mega versions of shared material. For reading operations, a 2 × 1 CMP is included that compares the tags from the OF stage [Td_{15}-Td_0] to those kept [Ts_{15}–Ts_0] in the cache lines.

The CU of the DPCAM design is a crucial component that is responsible for both managing the writing process and executing the replacement algorithm. Its goal is to generate an active signal in a cyclic pattern for each cache line. The control circuit is used to select which position to write the data to, as illustrated in **Figure 6**. The locations are chosen in order and are rewritten if needed to update their contents. This is accomplished by employing a collection of D Flip Flops (D-FF), each of which points

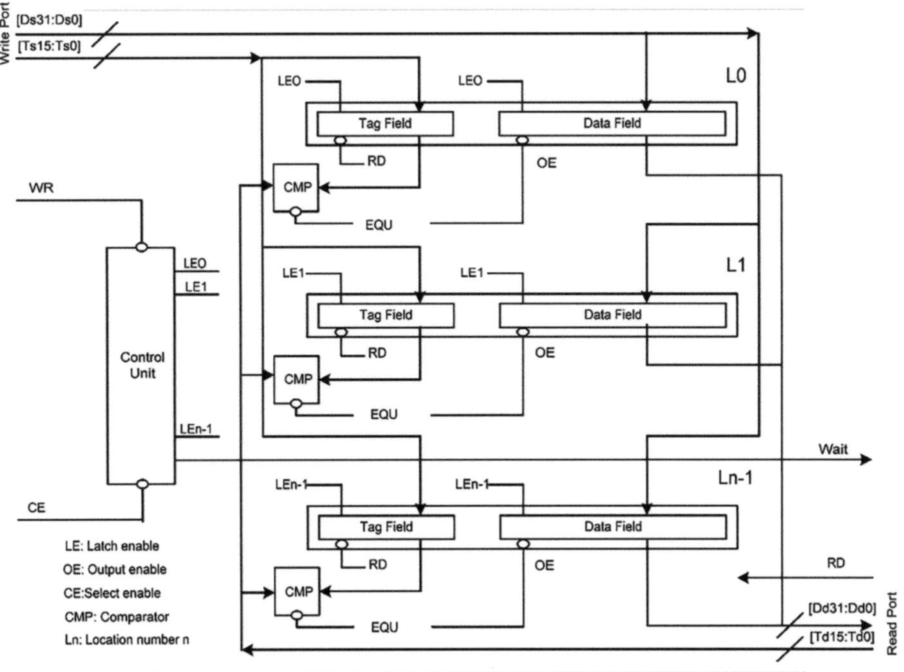

Figure 5.
DPCAM design.

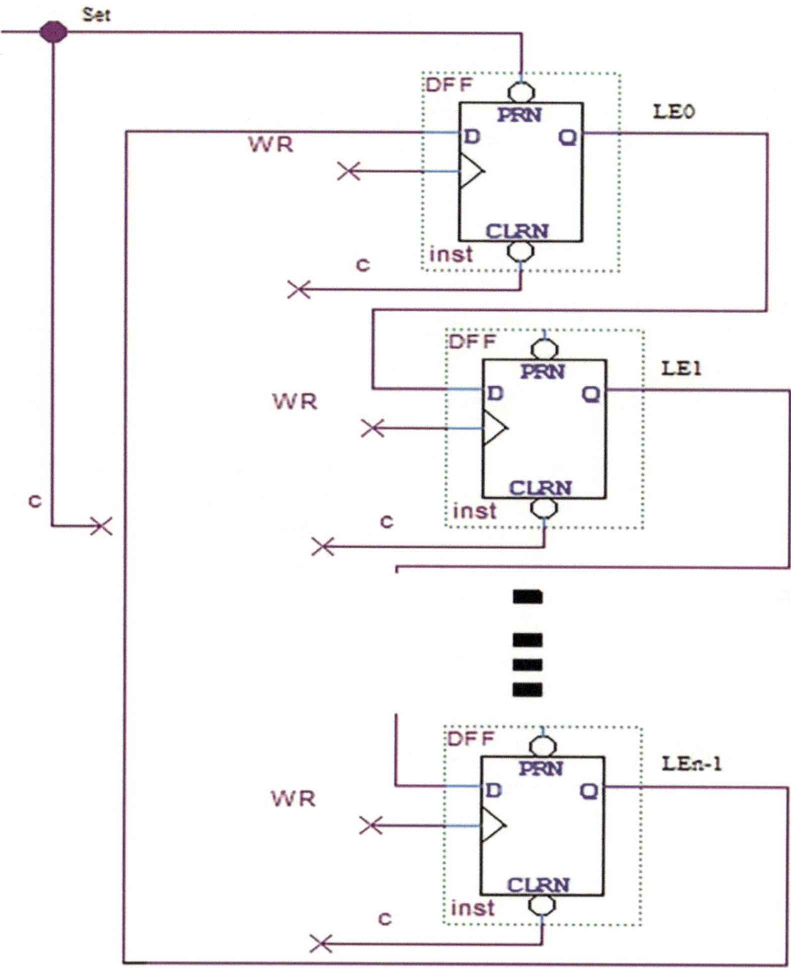

Figure 6.
Control unit.

to an associated DPCAM location. The first writing operation will be done on line L0 when the system is initially powered on, with the pointer indicating the first line, LE0. After writing to the current line, the pointer will shift to the next line and so on until the n − 1th line (Ln − 1) is reached.

The Write (WR) signal is transmitted by the CU from the first port (write port) in DPCAM, which is responsible for the writing operation. The stage buffer (SB) unit supplies the source data [Ds_{31}–Ds_0], the source tag [Ts_{15}–Ts_0], and an active low WR signal. The control circuit will then switch the LE to LE1 in order to write to line 1 whenever the WR signal reaches its negative edge (marking the end of the writing procedure). The output (OF) unit of the reading core will send an active high read (RD) signal and the tag destination (Td_{15}–Td_0) to all Tag Fields during the reading operation. The applied data's tag is compared to the tags kept in the memory lines. If a match is found, the CMP of each memory line will output an output enable (OE) signal. The data kept in the Data Field is then output *via* this signal to the destination data bus [Dd_{31}–Dd_0] for the reading core's OF unit to read. If the same memory address is requested for both reading and writing, the CU will give priority to the writing process and signal a WAIT to the reading operation. Both read and write ports can operate simultaneously if separate memory locations are requested for reading and writing, which lowers the cache access latency. While the SB unit of the writing core delivers the data [Ds_{31}–Ds_0] and the tag [Ts_{15}–Ts_0] to the precise position designated by the CU, the OF unit of the reading core concurrently transmits the destination tag [Td_{15}–Td_0] and the RD signal to all tag fields. This makes it possible to read the stored data from the target data bus [Dd_{31}-Dd_0].

The proposed architecture features a new, small DPCAM in place of the cache controller, which collects data from lower-level memory and increases access latency. Close-access data is stored in the main DPCAM module, as indicated in **Figure 7**, and far-access data is stored in the new module. As far-access data is used less often than near-access data, the far-access module is generally smaller. To illustrate, a four-core processor with a 64 KiB shared DPCAM can store 2 K operands, each composed of eight bytes of data plus a tag, before the data must be rebuilt.

The NFRA algorithm is implemented at the hardware level to reduce cache access latency. This technique involves writing a CU and pointer to position Lx, followed by instructions that write their operands to Lx + 1 to Ln − 1. After reaching the last position, the pointer returns to LE0 and overwrites the previous data and tags. Compared to a complex algorithm in the cache controller, this method is used for both near-access and far-access modules and has lower costs and access overhead. Moreover, it facilitates the storing, loading, and retrieving of near-access and far-access data/tags from various DPCAM modules [1]. According to the migration principle, the far-access module can be activated as needed and then switched to an inactive mode to conserve power when not in use [17, 18].

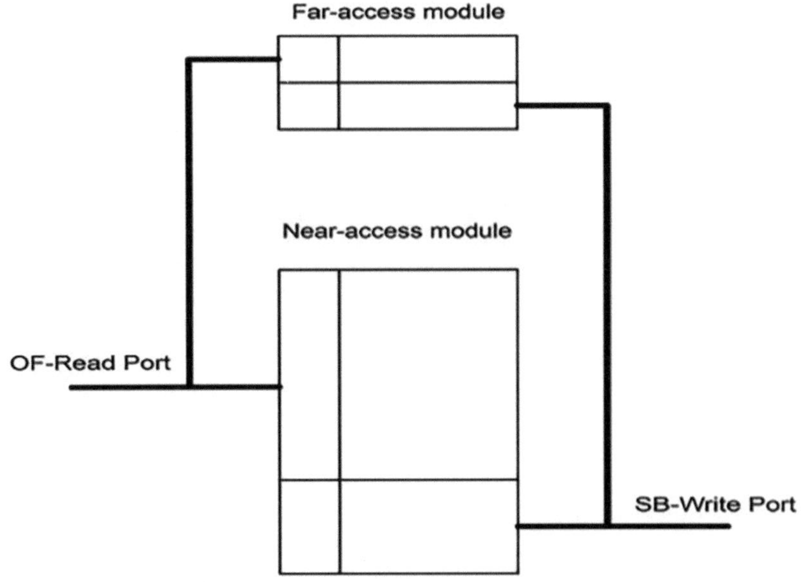

Figure 7.
Near-access, far-access DPCAM modules.

3. Implementation of the DPCAM and performance analysis

Quartus Prime 19.1 was utilized in the development, testing, and validation of DPCAM using Intel's FPGA Cyclone V family with 28 nm technology. ModelSim, Intel's design and simulation software, was employed to construct and examine DPCAM as a single memory [19]. In order to determine if DPCAM could replace the shared cache in the memory hierarchy of a multi-core CPU, two cores were utilized to measure the latency of read and write operations. Block schematics and Verilog Hardware Description Language (VHDL) files were implemented to develop the device, while Model Sim and Vector Wav File (VWF) were used for functional and timing simulation verification and debugging. The Power Analyzer Tool was also employed to evaluate the DPCAM's static and dynamic power consumption, and a tests-bench was created to simulate and analyze the latency of its reading and writing operations. To compare the performance of DPCAM, the SA cache, the most popular architecture type used as shared memory in multi-core computers, was employed [1, 2].

3.1 Functional assessments

The test-bench program was used to simulate the operations of the DPCAM and evaluate its latency and power usage. Firstly, it reset the CU and then created random 16-bit tags and 32-bit data to carry out write operations. Read/write signals were generated until the end of the simulation time and the output for the read operations was generated by comparing the 16-bit tags with the stored tags. It was used to compare the SA cache with the LRU replacement mechanism, and DPCAM with NFRA. The usage of the test-bench program is depicted in **Figure 8**. Through numerous simulations, it was demonstrated that the DPCAM's reading, writing, simultaneous read-write, CU, and replacement algorithms all operated as intended. **Figure 9** displays a 10 ns clock period of multiple clock cycles for reading and writing operations to the 64 KiB DPCAM. The CU was set to the first location in the first interval (0–10 ns) with the written data (out). The processor loaded the relevant tag (tagd) of the written data (outI) and used the RD signal to read the data from the desired out DPCAM location during the second interval (10–20 ns) using the WR signal. As soon as the RD signal went high, the processor output busses (outE) released the stored information. During interval 4 (30–40 ns), multiple DPCAM locations underwent read and write operations, with a write operation taking priority over the read operation. As a result, new data with a tag of [0]13 was written to the target location, while data previously written with a tag of [0]12 was accurately read. In interval 5 (40–50 ns), both read and write operations were performed on the same spot simultaneously.

3.2 Latency assessments

The performance of the DPCAM with regard to timing evaluation was evaluated using the Intel Quartus Prime Timing Analyzer. For each component of the design, this tool reports on all necessary data times, data arrival times, and clock arrival times using industry-standard constraint and analysis methodologies (Intel, 2021). The access latency for read and write operations in the DPCAM structure was measured using the Timing Analyzer, and real signal arrivals were compared to the design restrictions.

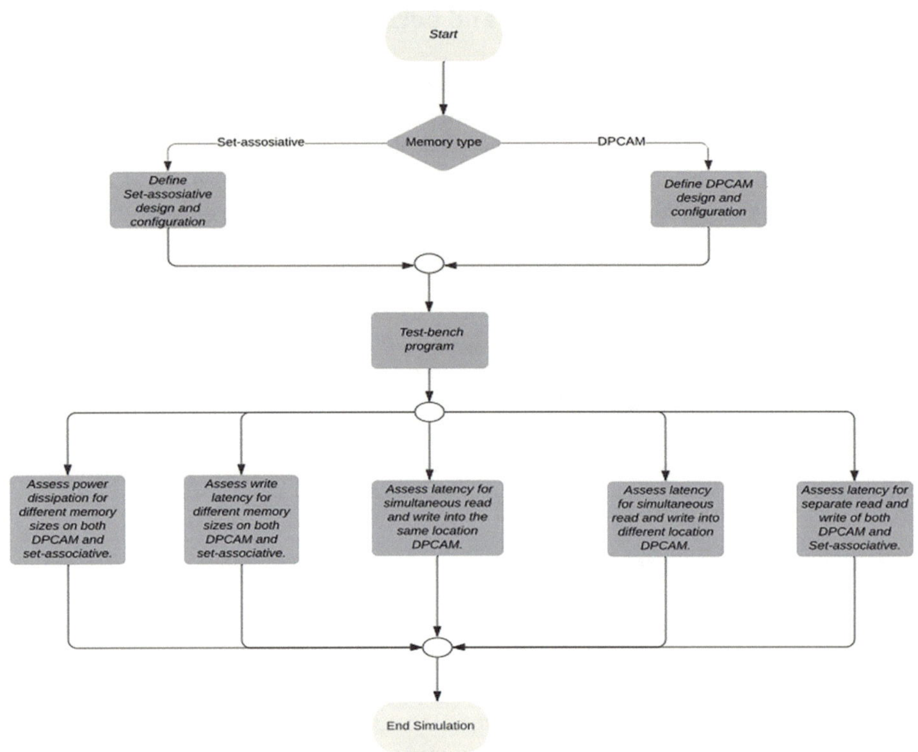

Figure 8.
Test-bench program.

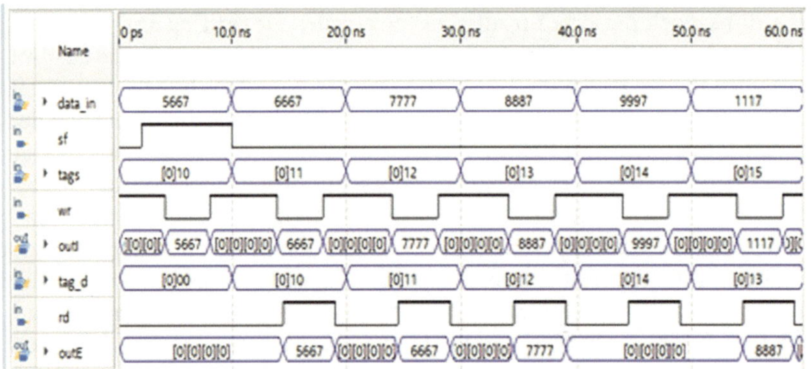

Figure 9.
Functional assessments.

To determine the delay of read and write operations, a 64 KiB near and distant DPCAM module timing simulation was performed using Intel's Cyclone V FPGA, as shown in **Figure 10**. After running the simulator 100 times, it was found that the average delay time for writing on DPCAM was 0.9529 ± 0.03393 ns. The WR signal was then turned off. The average latency for a read operation was found to be 1.1782 ± 0.08830 ns when the tag ([0]10) in the second interval was compared with

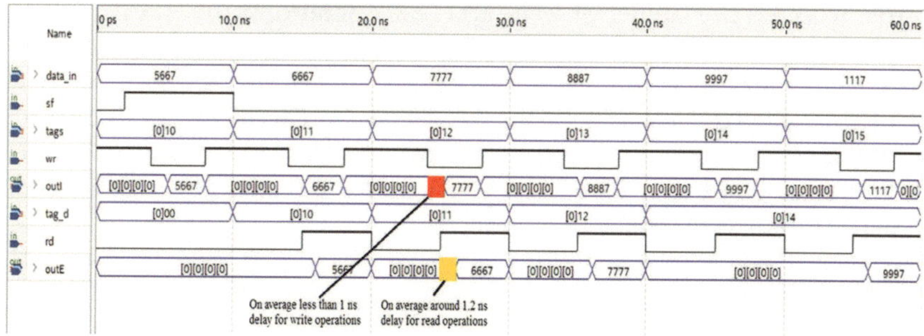

Figure 10.
Latency assessments.

the tags in all places with the RD signal. The fourth and fifth intervals were used to assess the latency of simultaneous read and write operations, and the average delay time was calculated to be the time between initiating a request for data and the actual data transfer for a single operation and the time between two requests for simultaneous write and read operations.

- $l_{SDL} = \max(l_{WR} + l_{RD})$ SDL is referred to simultaneous access RD/WR operations to the different memory lines
- $l_{SSL} = t_{CL} + l_{RD}$ SSL is referred to simultaneous access RD/WR operations to the same memory lines

Where l_{WR} is a latency of a write operation, l_{RD} is a latency of a read operation and t_{CL} is the cycle time.

Hundred simulations in two separate modes with write and read operations to unique or similar memory locations were run. The write and read latency for the latter mode were 0.98280.0412 ns and 1.2226 ± 0.09446 ns, respectively, with an overall latency of l_{SSL} = 11.2226 ± 0.09138 ns according to the T-test and 95% confidence interval. The average write latency was 1.9434 ± 0.0382 ns, and the average read latency was 2.15840.1056 ns, according to tests with a 64 KiB four-way SA cache. Unfortunately, due to SA cache limitations, simultaneous read and write operations could not be tested. The tested DPCAM has a lower read latency than the tested SA cache; this is because DPCAM compares the incoming tag directly with the stored tag, whereas SA caches must use an index to access the location with a tag to compare to, which increases the latency. Generally, a cache memory based on AM has a latency of around 2 ns for 64 KiB [20], 1.66 ns for AM with 1KiB, and 1.69 ns for 4-way set associative with 2 KiB, which is used in cache controllers [21]. However, the write latency for a cache memory based on AM typically exceeds 2 ns for 64KiB [20].

Using FPGA technology, a comparison of the write latency between a typical four-way set associative cache and a DPCAM design was made for equivalent-sized caches. Because the CU points directly to the memory location and does not need to generate the address of the following write site as is necessary for the AM cache memory, simulations have shown that DPCAM has a low and consistent write latency for variable memory sizes. As seen in **Figure 11** and **Table 1**, the write latency difference between DPCAM and the SA cache widens as memory capacity grows.

In order to assess the latency of write and read operations, the NFRA replacement method used by DPCAM and the LRU algorithm employed by the set associative cache memory were compared. The results showed that the set associative cache had an average latency of 0.9529 ± 0.03393 ns for a write operation and 1.1782 ± 0.08830 ns for a read operation, whereas the DPCAM recorded a lower access latency for a size of 64 KiB, with a latency of 1.9434 ± 0.0382 ns for a write operation and 2.1584 ± 0.1056 ns for a read operation.

3.2.1 Descriptive statistics

About 100 times were spent running the simulator with various test-bench values, documenting the latency for write and read operations as well as for simultaneous read and write operations into distinct memory locations and the same memory location. In order to determine the minimum, maximum, mean, and standard error for DPCAM and SA architecture, data analysis was done using SPSS and *T*-test tools. **Table 2** displays descriptive data for write latency in DPCAM, **Table 3** describes descriptive statistics for read latency, **Table 4** describes descriptive statistics for simultaneous read and write operations into distinct memory locations, and **Table 5** describes descriptive statistics for simultaneous read and write operations into the same memory regions. Similar descriptive statistics for write and read latency in set associative are shown in **Tables 6** and 7. The write and read operations between DPCAM and SA memory were

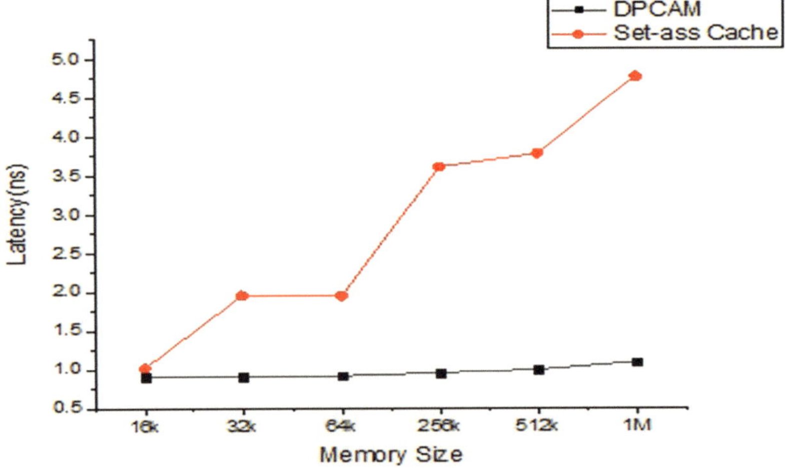

Figure 11.
Write access latency (ns).

Size	DPCAM	Cache	Size	DPCAM	Cache
16 K	0.90	1.02	256 K	0.95	3.60
32 K	0.90	1.95	512 K	0.99	3.77
64 K	0.91	1.94	1 M	1.09	4.76

Table 1.
Write operation access latency (ns).

	N	Minimum	Maximum	Mean	Std.	
	Statistic	Statistic	Statistic	Statistic	Std. error	Statistic
Write	100	0.89	1.10	0.9529	0.00339	0.03393
DPCAM	100					

Table 2.
Descriptive statistics for write latency in DPCAM.

	N	Minimum	Maximum	Mean	Std.	
	Statistic	Statistic	Statistic	Statistic	Std. Error	Statistic
Read DPCAM	100	1	1.35	1.1782	0.00883	0.0883
	100					

Table 3.
Descriptive statistics for read latency in DPCAM.

	N	Minimum	Maximum	Mean	Std.	
	Statistic	Statistic	Statistic	Statistic	Std. error	Statistic
Write/ read different location DPCAM	100 100	1	1.40	1.2262	0.00945	0.0945

Table 4.
Descriptive statistics for simultaneous access latency Rd/Wr operations in the same DPCAM location.

	N	Minimum	Maximum	Mean	Std.	
	Statistic	Statistic	Statistic	Statistic	Std. Error	Statistic
Write/ read same location DPCAM	100 100	0.91	1.10	0.9828	0.00412	0.0412

Table 5.
Descriptive statistics for simultaneous access latency Rd/Wr operations in the same DPCAM location.

compared using the T-test, and it was discovered that DPCAM had lower write and read latencies than those of SA memory with a 95% confidence interval.

3.3 Estimation of a power dissipation

Power management is essential to achieving better size, performance, and affordability while maintaining a high power density as chip technology continues to get smaller. The Quartus simulator's Power Analyzer Tool estimates power dissipation with an accuracy of 10% to make sure components use the right amount of power and enhance the design [22]. Based on the waveform file generated by Model Sim while

	N	Minimum	Maximum	Mean	Std.	
	Statistic	Statistic	Statistic	Statistic	Std. error	Statistic
Write SA	100	1.88	2.10	1.9434	0.00382	0.0382
	100					

Table 6.
Descriptive statistics for write latency in SA.

	N	Minimum	Maximum	Mean	Std.	
	Statistic	Statistic	Statistic	Statistic	Std. error	Statistic
Read SA	100	1.95	2.35	2.1584	0.01056	0.1056
	100					

Table 7.
Descriptive statistics for read latency in SA.

simulating the script with the DPCAM design at the gate level, the Power Analyzer Tool was used to assess static, dynamic, I/O, and overall power consumption.

This section compares and evaluates the power dissipation of DPCAM and four-way SA caches with various memory capacities. The DPCAM dissipates electricity through near-far access modules. Static power, which is the leakage power of the functional unit on the FPGA excluding the I/O port, is the thermal energy used on the chip. Dynamic power is the amount of energy used when a unit is in use or when a signal is changing. The pins, which power components on and off-chip and have an impact on dynamic power, produce I/O power [22].

In **Figure 12**, the static, dynamic, and I/O power dissipation of DPCAMs and SA caches can be compared. From **Figure 12a**, it is evident that DPCAMs have a higher static power dissipation than SA caches. This is because increasing the size of the DPCAMs leads to the complexity of the hardware created by the CU and internal wires covering a larger surface, resulting in an increased static power dissipation. **Tables 8** and **9** further provide a comparison of the static, dynamic, I/O, and total power dissipation of DPCAMs and SA caches, respectively, for different sizes. **Figure 12b** compares the dynamic power dissipation of DPCAM and SA. It can be observed that when the size is less than 512 K, the dynamic power of DPCAM is similar to that of SA. However, after 256 K, it increases significantly due to

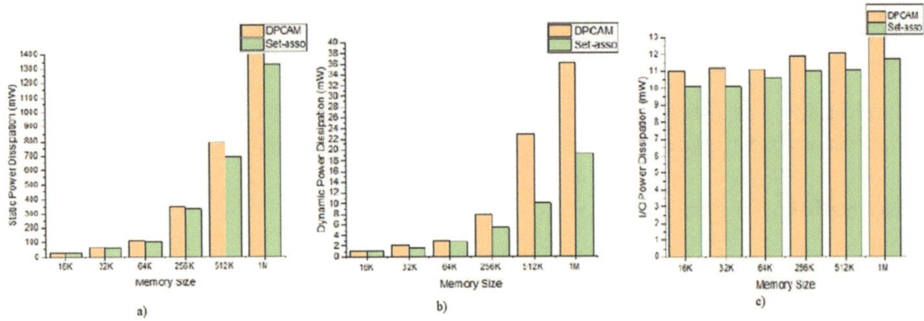

Figure 12.
Power dissipation with variation in memory size: (a) Compared the static power dissipation between DPCAM and SA. (b) Compared dynamic power dissipation. (c) It is compared I/O power dissipation.

	Power in milliwatts (mW)			
Size	**Static**	**Dynamic**	**I/O**	**Total**
16 K	32.214	1.13	11	44.344
32 K	64.33	2.14	11.21	77.68
64 K	107.57	2.99	11.10	121.66
256 K	349.5	7.98	11.88	369.28
512 K	796.2	22.90	12.07	831.17
1 M	1411.10	39.26	13.21	1463.57

Table 8.
DPCAM power dissipation.

	Power in (mW)			
Size	**Static**	**Dynamic**	**I/O**	**Total**
16 K	28.9166	1.12	10.1	40.1366
32 K	57.33	1.62	10.1	69.05
64 K	99.41	2.79	10.6	112.8
256 K	334.750	5.48	11	351.23
512 K	696.261	10.021	11.025	771.307
1 M	1325.310	19.28	11.737	1356.326

Table 9.
SA memory power dissipation.

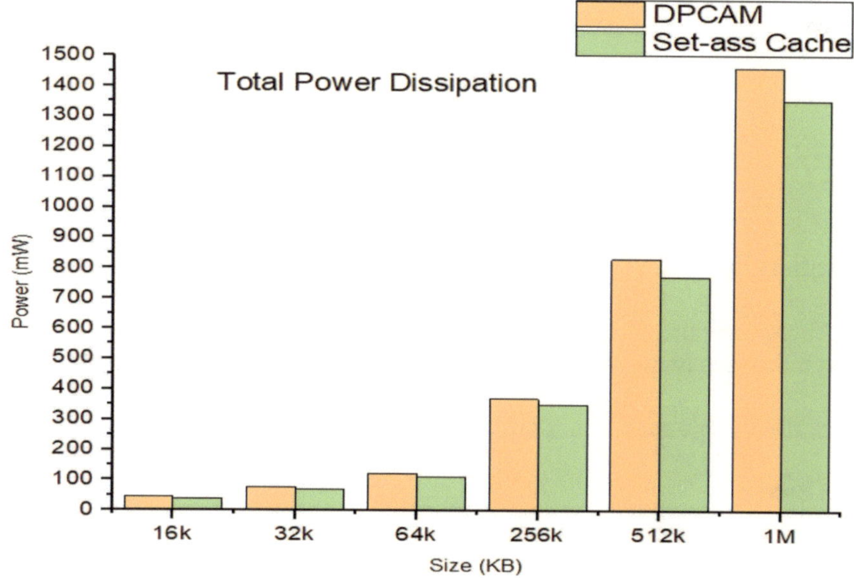

Figure 13.
Total power dissipation with variation in size.

numerous active locations being accessed during read operations. **Figure 12c**'s comparison of I/O power dissipation reveals that the DPCAM's I/O power is comparable to the SA with varied sizes, since the off-chip pins remain constant regardless of the internal memory capacity. **Figure 13** indicates that the total power used by DPCAM is only marginally higher than that of the SA cache, at around 7%. This small increase in power dissipation can be managed through power-saving techniques, such as those found in refs. [17, 18, 23–25], thus not prohibiting the adoption of DPCAM in multi-core systems.

4. Conclusion

A design of a special purpose-shared memory architecture based on CAM and a replacement algorithm has been presented in this chapter. This architecture was designed to enable multi-core processors to access the cache memory with lower latency than the traditional SA cache. It should be stressed that while all of the previous replacement algorithms do not make use of cache hardware architecture, they increase non-computational times for updating the location and introduce new access overhead. In order to lower the cost overhead and complexity of the cache controller, Near-Far Access Replacement Algorithm (NFRA) is also suggested and implemented as a hardware component inside the DPCAM module.

Testing the design on a Cyclone V Intel FPGA showed that the DPCAM could replace the shared cache in the memory hierarchy of a multi-core processor. The DPCAM had an average latency of 1.2 ± 0.09138 ns for reading operations and 0.9679 ± 0.0642 for writing operations, which is better than other types of shared memory. Furthermore, the access latency for a write operation was almost the same regardless of the memory size. Although the DPCAM consumes more power than the SA memory, some power-saving techniques can be used to reduce this amount.

Author details

Allam Abumwais* and Mahmoud Obaid
Computer Systems Engineering, Arab American University, Jenin, Palestine

*Address all correspondence to: allam.abumwais@aaup.edu

References

[1] Patterson DA, Hennessy JL. Computer Organization and Design The Hardware Software Interface. 2nd ed. United States: Morgan kaufmann; 2020

[2] Stallings W. Computer organization and architecture. In: Wu H-K, Lee SW-Y, Chang H-Y, J, editors. Designing For Performance. 9th ed. United States: Pearson Education; 2013

[3] Karam R, Puri R, Ghosh S, Bhunia S. Emerging trends in design and applications of memory-based computing and content-addressable memories. Proceedings of the IEEE. 2015;**103**(8):1311-1330

[4] Olanrewaju RF, et al. A study on performance evaluation of conventional cache replacement algorithms: a review. In: 2016 Fourth International Conference on Parallel, Distributed and Grid Computing (PDGC). IEEE; 2016

[5] Priya BK, Kumar S, Begum BS, Ramasubramanian N. Cache lifetime enhancement technique using hybrid cache-replacement-policy. Microelectronics Reliability. 2019;**97**:1-15

[6] Abumwais A, Ayyad A. The MPCAM based multi-core processor architecture: A contention free architecture. WSEAS Transactions on Electronics. 2018;**9**:105-111

[7] Irfan M, Cheung RC, Ullah Z. High-throughput re-configurable content-addressable memory on FPGAs. In: Proceedings of the 2019 International Conference on Information Technology and Computer Communications. 2019

[8] Abumwais A, Amirjanov A, Uyarl K, Eleyat M. Dual-port content addressable memory for cache memory applications. Computer, Material & Continua. 2021;**70**(3):4583-4597

[9] Abumwais A, Obaid M. Shared cache based on content addressable memory in a multi-core architecture. CMC-Computers, Materials & Continua. 2023;**74**(3):4951-4963

[10] Cheriton DR. U.S. Patent No. 9,111,013. Washington, DC: U.S. Patent and Trademark Office; 2015

[11] Nakaike T, Odaira R, Gaudet M, Michael MM, Tomari H. Quantitative comparison of hardware transactional memory for Blue Gene/Q, zEnterprise EC12, Intel Core, and POWER8. ACM SIGARCH Computer Architecture News. 2015;**43**(3S):144-157

[12] Papagiannopoulou D, Marongiu A, Moreshet T, Benini L, Herlihy M, Bahar RI. Hardware transactional memory exploration in coherence-free many-core architectures. International Journal of Parallel Programming. 2018;**46**:1304-1328

[13] Bhattacharya D, Bhoj AN, Jha NK. Design of efficient content addressable memories in high-performance FinFET technology. IEEE Transactions on Very Large Scale Integration (VLSI) Systems. 2014;**23**(5):963-967

[14] Imani M, et al. Digitalpim: digital-based processing in-memory for big data acceleration. In: Proceedings of the 2019 on Great Lakes Symposium on VLSI. 2019

[15] Martyshkin AI, Salnikov II, Pashchenko DV, Trokoz DA. Associative co-processor on the basis of programmable logical integrated circuits for special purpose computer systems. In: 2018 Global Smart Industry Conference (GloSIC). IEEE; Nov 2018. pp. 1-5

[16] Ullah I, Ullah Z, Lee JA. Ee-tcam: An energy-efficient sram-based tcam on fpga. Electronics. 2018;7(9):186

[17] Luo JY, Cheng HY, Lin C, Chang DW. TAP: reducing the energy of asymmetric hybrid last-level cache via thrashing aware placement and migration. IEEE Transactions on Computers. 2019;**68**(12):1704-1719

[18] Ofori-Attah E, Bhebhe W, Opoku Agyeman M. Architectural techniques for improving the power consumption of noc-based cmps: A case study of cache and network layer. Journal of Low Power Electronics and Applications. 2017;**7**(2):14

[19] Cyclone V Device Overview. Available from: https://www.intel.com/content/www/us/en/docs/programmable/683694/current/cyclone-v-device-overview.html

[20] Cargnini LV, Torres L, Brum RM, Senni S, Sassatelli G. Embedded memory hierarchy exploration based on magnetic random access memory. Journal of Low Power Electronics and Applications. 2014;**4**(3):214-230

[21] Chauan P, Singh G, Singh GJ. Cache controller for 4-way set-associative cache memory. 2015;**129(1):8887**

[22] Quartus Handbook. Volume 3: Verification. Available from: https://www.mouser.com/pdfdocs/qts-qps-5v3.pdf

[23] Adegbija T, Gordon-Ross A. PhLock: A cache energy saving technique using phase-based cache locking. IEEE Transactions on Very Large Scale Integration (VLSI) Systems. 2017;**26**(1):110-121

[24] Park J, Lee M, Kim S, Ju M, Hong J. MH cache: A multi-retention STT-RAM-based low-power last-level cache for mobile hardware rendering systems. ACM Transactions on Architecture and Code Optimization (TACO). 2019;**16**(3):1-26

[25] Rossi D et al. Exploiting aging benefits for the design of reliable drowsy cache memories. 2017;**37**(7):1345-1357